MARIA GOOS

Cloaca

faber and faber

First published in 2004
by Faber and Faber Limited
3 Queen Square London WC1N 3AU

Typeset by Country Setting, Kingsdown, Kent CT14 8ES
Printed in England by Mackays of Chatham plc, Chatham, Kent

Maria Goos is hereby identified as author
of this work in accordance with Section 77 of the
Copyright, Designs and Patents Act 1988

All rights whatsoever in this work are strictly reserved.
Applications for permission for any use whatsoever including
performance rights must be made in advance, prior to any such
proposed use, to Kik Productions, P.O. Box 13120, 3507 LC,
Utrecht, The Netherlands. No performance may be given
unless a licence has first been obtained

*This book is sold subject to the condition that it shall not, by
way of trade or otherwise, be lent, resold, hired out or otherwise
circulated without the publisher's prior consent in any form of
binding or cover other than that in which it is published and
without a similar condition including this condition being
imposed on the subsequent purchaser*

A CIP record for this book
is available from the British Library

ISBN 0-571-22684-1

2 4 6 8 10 9 7 5 3 1

Cloaca was first presented in Britain at The Old Vic, London, on 16 September 2004. The cast, in order of appearance, was as follows:

Pieter Stephen Tompkinson
Jan Hugh Bonneville
Tom Adrian Lukis
Maarten Neil Pearson
Woman Ingeborga Dapkunaite

Director Kevin Spacey
Designer Robert Jones
Lighting Mark Henderson
Sound Fergus O'Hare
Assistant Director Jeremy Whelehan
Literal translation by P. C. Evans

Producer David Liddiment
Executive Producer Colin Ingram
Production Manager Dominic Fraser
Casting Director Joyce Nettles
Company Stage Manager Jane Semark

Author's Note

My thanks to David Liddiment
for his tremendous help with the translation

Characters

Pieter
Jan
Tom
Maarten
Woman

CLOACA

Scene: a large spacious loft with a view over Amsterdam.
Pieter is on the telephone, wearing what he sleeps in:
a T-shirt and boxer shorts. Only a table lamp is burning.

Pieter Actually, I think you've got the wrong number.
(. . .) Yes, that's my name, yes. (. . .) Yes, I do, yes. (. . .)
Yes, that's right, yes, that's right too. (. . .) Yes, that's
quite true. That's correct. (. . .) Quite. Yes, that's right.
Are you sure it's me you want to talk to? (. . .) What
do you mean, naive!? I'm doing my level best not to get
angry with you. Because you are taking quite a liberty . . .
though . . . naive . . . that's not such a bad thing . . .
actually it's quite a compliment, but not coming from you,
even though I don't know you personally . . . you . . .
you . . . you . . . (. . .) No, that's what I'm saying! If
you'd only bother to listen to me for a second then you
would realise that's what I just said. (. . .) Look, you
and I have never met, so shall we simply hang up? That
seems like a good idea to me. (. . .) No. No . . . wait
wait wait . . . no, no, no . . . now you are turning the
whole thing around. Now you are just turning the whole
thing around . . . no, no, no . . . you . . . you . . . you . . .
goodnight!

> *Pieter puts the phone down. Stands stunned. As if he's*
> *forgotten to breathe. As the silence continues, he goes*
> *and sits on the couch as though hypnotised. Picks up*
> *the phone again quickly when it rings and immediately*
> *starts talking.*

You're asking me . . . at least if I understand you
correctly . . . but that's just not possible . . . Forgive me

if I've got the wrong end of the stick but let me play back to you what I think you are saying . . . You want me to return all my birthday presents from the last twenty-one years. I think that's what you said. Please tell me I'm mistaken. (. . .) No, I . . . if I can interrupt you, if I can interrupt you there, if I can interrupt you there . . . If I can just interrupt you there, it is actually the case that . . . (*suddenly extremely angry*) I should have known better is not the point. You should have known better! (. . .) No! No! Now come on, no! (. . .) You . . . (. . .) Yes . . . but you . . . (. . .) Yes . . . (. . .) Yes. (. . .) But you . . . (. . .) You . . . but can I just get back to the facts of the matter? (. . .) Yes, that is right . . . But can I just get back to the facts? You call me out of the blue . . . after ten o'clock at night, which is very impolite, I'm completely unprepared . . . nobody has ever mentioned a thing to me about it . . . and out of the blue you call . . . I don't even know you . . . (. . .) Yes, of course I know who you are. You're my boss's boss! You've been the director of culture, welfare and greater metropolitan policy for the last year and a half and before that you were in recreation and leisure for fifteen years. I've seen you at the Christmas parties. But getting back to the matter in hand . . . you . . . that isn't something you can just ask me. You just can't ask that.

And suddenly he hangs up again. Is seized by a brief violent crying fit. When the telephone rings again.

You can't actually do that! You can't just do that. I can't be made to give back everything, that's just not possible. (. . .) Because they're mine. Mine! Not the council's, not yours, mine! (. . .) It is legal! Totally legal! (. . .) From my colleagues! All of them. The whole department! Everyone! For the first seven years there were five, and in the last few years eleven, I count the two juniors as one because they're part-time, one is fifty per cent in culture and the other fifty per cent in welfare. (. . .) It was all completely above board and with the full knowledge of everyone concerned! And Vermeulen, the head of department, knows all about it. And so if there's anything you want to ask, you can just call Jacques Vermeulen, who you must know well because you swim with him three times a week, and go cycling with him on the weekend. If it isn't too windy. You're a pair of queens and you don't even know it. (. . .) A pair of queens. (*He puts the phone down. Realises what he has said and is amazed.*) Queens?

The telephone rings again.

Forget what I said about queens. I'm sorry. (. . .) I didn't mean . . . (. . .) Who am I speaking to?

It is a different caller. Pieter turns towards the door, and to his astonishment sees the man who is now on the telephone standing there wih a mobile. The man has a bloody nose and is carrying a bag and a suitcase.

Jan Just popped in. For a laugh.

Darkness.

Pieter is sitting, shaken, on the couch; Jan is standing in the room. Both have a bottle of beer. Jan's coat is lying on the floor near his bag and suitcase. He has a wad of cotton wool in each nostril and he wears jogging trousers.

Jan Rows, rows. rows. Row. It's such a loaded word. Row . . . but . . . it's a release, maybe. I was thinking: before things get really . . . unpleasant . . . because, well . . . you know how it goes . . . you've been together for twenty years or so . . . eh . . . and by then the day-to-day pleasantries have got a bit strained . . . Not that I've got a shit marriage . . . we do still have lots of fun together. Well. 'Fun' is maybe a bit . . . 'fun' isn't . . . fun fun. Sometimes we can really have a good laugh together . . . and it's just like everyone says . . . too busy, a bit bored, you have everything, yet it's kind of empty . . . Sex is . . . way down the agenda. . . Still . . . it's not that bad really . . . Unrelenting. Stiff. Uptight, really. God, is that woman uptight!

Pieter Who?

Jan Conny, of course.

Pieter Oh, come on. Conny isn't the least bit uptight.

Jan That woman's got a picture in her head of what a good marriage should be and I just don't live up to it, less and less so, actually, because, Pieter, and you won't believe this, a good marriage stands or falls on whether you bring home the right brand of cereal, and how in a moment of weakness you happen to describe your retirement. You don't understand me, do you? It's not really something that anyone can understand. Actually it is impossible to understand that a man and a woman who were once young, who loved each other, who laughed together . . . who liked just being together. How something like that can grow . . . wither . . . and die . . . it's beyond understanding.

God. I was thirsty. So I get up and go downstairs. Glass of water, sit on my own for a while. The garden doors open. Lovely. Little bit of air. A bit of peace. But she comes after me. In my own house. She stands in the hall and screams at me in the kitchen: 'I will never forgive you!' She says: 'I will never be able to forgive you.' Well . . . you'd never guess, never, really . . . what it was all about. But I found myself standing there with a meat fork

6

in my hands. With a meat fork. It was not dinner time, there were no guests, no joint, no gravy, no party, no Christmas, the table bare and me with a meat fork. Can you see me standing there, Piet? Conny in pyjamas, me with a meat fork? I suddenly had a vision. I thought: I'll hoist her up and skewer her like this with her head pinned to the coat rack. With a coat hook in that soft little cleft here . . . under the skull . . . and then I'll finish her off with the meat fork. Well . . . nonsense, nonsense of course, you just don't do it, do you? But why not? you ask yourself. Why?

Pieter No, I don't ask myself that at all. What's more, I don't even want to know.

Jan She was lying in bed, with her back turned to me, and she asked, 'How do you see the future?' A trick question, but I didn't realise it at the time. So I told her what I honestly dreamt of: a boat, a little house in France and an apartment on the canal. Explain – she wanted me to explain. Why, I thought – naive prick that I am – a boat to . . . well . . . to go sailing, of course . . . a little farm, my books inside, and outside my own small but exclusive vineyard . . . and an apartment in town for a bit of life. Films, concerts. She says: 'Where do I fit in? I don't fit into it anywhere.' . . . So, one minute you're standing by the sink with a glass of water and the next you're in the hall holding a bloody meat fork. Anyway. It all turned out all right. I grabbed some things, pulled my coat on and left. I know what you're thinking: How did you end up with that nose, then?

But Pieter wasn't asking himself that at all.

Because I pulled that fucking case off the shelf above the garage door without turning the light on. That's how. Because, of course, I know where the cases are in my own house. I could feel I'd got hold of it, next thing

7

I knew I'm flat on my back with Bram's snowboard and two old hockey sticks on top of me. Now who would put a snowboard and two hockey sticks on top of the suitcases? That . . . sort of thoughtlessness is hard to reconcile with what in essence are intelligent people, because Conny and the kids, all five of them, they're smart, they're not stupid . . . yet they behave no better than a tribe of . . . Neanderthals. They live like pigs and they're oblivious to it. Pens. I must have taken home thousands of pens from party conferences, but if I need to write down a telephone number, I can't find a pen anywhere. In that whole fucking house, not one single pen!

I'm only human too. I ride a bicycle and so from time to time I need a bicycle pump. Over the last twenty years I must have bought at least six bicycle pumps . . . yet never, and I mean never, have I been able to find a bicycle pump when I needed one. What do they do with these fucking pumps? You can never find a bloody thing in that house. She calls it 'cosy', I call it a fucking tip. Not one sock matches another, there are mice in the hall cupboard, which no poison may ever be used on. No, do you know what they do now? Conny and the children? Knock. On the cupboard door. Knock! So that the mice can run away before they open it, otherwise Catweazle will eat them. Our cat, you know? The idiot with epilepsy. And he can't have an injection either, no, because he's been with her since college! Twenty-four that bastard is! Pees on the doormat, usually on the daily paper or my post, but a merciful little injection . . . oh no! In the kitchen there's a leak, with a bowl under it since I don't know when. Now why not ring a plumber? Because Catweazle is used to drinking out of that bowl. Do you understand that logic? I come home at night . . . fancy a few crisps . . . Gone! . . . Or soggy. Bit of chocolate, you think . . . empty wrappers. A tin full of empty wrappers. I'll just have a cheese sandwich then, dry, of course, because the bread's been left out, and a quick zap . . . remote's gone. Three remotes! Three telephones too. I had to make this urgent call last night. Do you know where I finally found the telephone? In the bikini bottom of Teddy's polar bear, which she was sleeping on in her bunk bed. If it's 'anything goes' for everyone else . . . why not for me? Why can't I dream about a boat and a little farm? A place where everything is just as it should be.

Jan goes and sits on the couch with Pieter. Pats him on the thigh.

Jan Pieter.

Pieter Jan.

Jan God, Pieter. It's great that I can stay.

Pieter I haven't said that you could.

Jan I can't go to a hotel.

Pieter It's okay, you can stay. I just hadn't said it yet.

Jan There'd be talk, me in a hotel, now. It's great that I can stay. I always knew I could count on you.

Pieter Jan, I've just had a call . . .

Jan As long as the cabinet's still up in the air, one false move could be disastrous, Pieter.

Pieter A very unpleasant call.

Jan Until the appointments are confirmed I can't go to a hotel.

Pieter You don't have to go to a hotel!

Jan That would be out of the question. Absolutely impossible. Am I crazy? To come and stay with a homosexual now?

Pieter That new cabinet . . . it could still take weeks.

Jan Oh, no. A couple of days. No more. There've been some whispers, of course. And well, you know how it is . . . they can't ignore me. It's a very natural progression. From deputy vice-chairman to cabinet minister, unfortunately, for a different party than I'd planned. So . . . yes . . . the cabinet, yes. Soon. Peculiar call?

Pieter considers showing Jan the door.

Pieter . . . 'Unpleasant' call. They want me to return my paintings.

Jan Oh, something at work.

Pieter A communication course wouldn't go amiss if you become minister.

Jan Department of Employment, Social Services, the Treasury or the Foreign Office. Preferably the FO. I'd say thanks but no thanks to any other post, they'd be taking the piss. Being abroad a lot seems a very attractive option for the next few years, especially now that everything seems to be buggered at home.

Pieter When were you here last?

Jan Exactly. God, a family can ruin your social life. (*He pats Pieter on the thigh again.*) Pieter –

Pieter Jan.

Jan We should have done this much more often, don't you think? Just us. When do I ever get to see you these days? A party here, a reception there. We used to go to the movies together. That's something else we don't do any more. Why not? Do you want to go to a movie?

Pieter Now?

Jan Yes! Now!

Pieter Do you know a good lawyer?

Jan Unbelievable, eh? You let the best things, the things that it's really all about, you let them slip through your fingers. A jog around the park? Tomorrow morning? Why did we ever stop doing that . . .?

Pieter We didn't stop doing that, you just stopped coming. I still run there. Do you know a good lawyer?

Jan Do you know, I seriously thought of asking you to be the godfather to my youngest?

Pieter Bram?

Jan Teddy! Teddy's the youngest. Or did Bram come after . . . I can't think straight.

Pieter Bram. Bram is the youngest. Laura, Micha, Teddy, Bram. Do you know a good lawyer?

Jan 'We' know a good lawyer.

Darkness.

Jan has gone, as have his things. Pieter is standing in the middle of the room and looks towards the door. In the doorway an enthusiastic man is standing with his arms spread wide.

Tom This is so nice. This is wonderful. Oh, Pieter, Pieter. (*He embraces Pieter emotionally.*) Of course I want to help you. Of course I'm going to help you . . . oh, this is great. Something at your work? I didn't really get it all on the phone. Oh . . . Pieter . . . Piet, Piet, Piet . . . something at work, eh? I was really . . . the fact that you asked me . . . I mean . . . so many lawyers . . . and so many better than me . . . and . . . who have a less problematic

past. I'm completely over it now . . . that's something
I admire so much in you . . . that you're willing to take
a chance on me . . . I may take a little while to get back
into it again . . . that I've been debarred makes it a little
more complicated, but we'll sort all that out. I'm really
up for it. I'm going to sink my teeth into it. This'll be my
first case, since the clinic.

Pieter Since the clinic. Clinic?

Tom Pieter . . . Pieter.

Pieter It was actually Jan's idea, to ask you, I didn't
know anything about a clinic.

Tom Jan! Jesus, Jan, yeah. Janny. Was it Jan's idea? He's
going to be a cabinet minister. But we knew that twenty
years ago, eh? Funny, eh? He's totally unsuited for it! The
whole party hates him, did you know that? So Jan
recommended me?

Pieter Actually, I thought the two of you regularly . . .

Tom Before I was in hospital! Everything is different
now, Piet. Two months in the madhouse and everything
has changed for ever. But Jan recommended me. That's a
surprise.

Pieter I didn't know about it, Tom. I thought you were . . .
just busy . . . maybe off somewhere. Hospital? Why
didn't I know about it?

Tom Funny, eh? Jan a cabinet minister. And why?
Because he has no shame. He is so brilliant at appearing
brilliant. The Labour Party was totally unprepared for it.
They were completely dazzled by him. That's why he'd
been with them since he was sixteen.

Pieter Tom . . . just start at the beginning.

Tom Because essentially he's a Conservative of course.
We play squash. Jan and I. In the afternoon, opposite the

ministry. Twice a week up until six months ago, Piet. Sweating, laughing. I was still walking the corridors of the Treasury in a bespoke pinstripe suit, with a leather-bound case that cost eleven hundred guilders, just buzzing, because when a legal egg had to be cracked it was me they called . . . I was good . . . I was very good. (*suddenly extremely dejected*) I was good, wasn't I? The RAM case.

Pieter Ram?

Tom The copyright for RAM. The big case I won . . . remember?

Pieter What do you mean, clinic? What did you do, then? And tell me calmly, calmly.

Tom I had just won that RAM case, we were drinking a toast in the bar of Des Indes, and twenty-four hours later I was walking through the centre of Barcelona in my underpants. I've no idea how I got there. Next thing I was in the institution.

Pieter What in God's name had you done or taken?

Tom Just what I'd been doing for twenty years. Go, go, go!

Pieter Go, go, go, but how . . .

Tom I remember that I thought I was acting in a film. So when they beat me up in Barcelona I didn't do anything to stop them.

Pieter This doesn't make any sense. I . . . can't follow it.

Tom I vaguely remember that I had to be beaten up because it was in the script. So. Fine. Finished. Over. Done. Something at work?

Pieter Yes. You're talking about . . . an institution . . . a clinic . . . an institution? Tom . . . no bollocks now . . .

I want a straight story. All the facts in chronological order.

Tom Half the world is manic, or depressed *and* manic, Pieter, that's a fact. But in my case, because of that tapeworm coke which crawled up my nose every day, one moment I was fine, the next, snap, I was gone, completely crazy. (*Suddenly he's finished. Deep sigh*) It was really awful.

Pieter I thought you were just busy with something, and we've often not seen each other for months at a time . . .

Tom Oh, but I'm not blaming you. It's just that I didn't want to. See anyone.

Pieter No, you wouldn't want to, of course. Of course you wouldn't want to. But I still should have been there.

Tom I couldn't remember anyone I should have called. Everything was . . . gone.

Pieter You must have felt very alone.

Tom Yes. It was a long, chilling descent. Yes. I'm back now, though.

Pieter I thought: I don't need to ask Tom. He'll have no time.

Tom 'This lavish coffee table is an eye-catcher in any living room. Veneered with an attractive fossil-stone finish.'

Pieter Hospitalised!

Tom This is what I do, you see. Do you understand?

Pieter No!

Tom Since I left the institution this is what I do. I'm still a lawyer, of course, and it's wonderful that the two of you have a case for me, but at the moment, I'm a copywriter.

Pieter How long is it since you and Jan last saw each other?

Tom For catalogues. 'Not to be missed! A pullover with a daring, low-cut neckline. Ideal as a twin-set in combination with waistcoat number one, or the very latest, over a blouse.' It's all delivered via the computer, I don't have to leave the house, and I get to think about something else for a couple of hours a day other than the best way of doing myself in. It's really refreshing.

Pieter So you are still a bit unstable.

Tom No, oh no. You shouldn't take that bit about my doing myself in too seriously. To me it's something to hold on to like everybody knowing they'll go on holiday three weeks every year.

Pieter I really didn't know anything about it, Tom. Partly because . . . and I don't know why, actually . . . we stopped going to concerts together. Both busy, I suppose. I honestly didn't know anything about it. And I don't think Jan knows either. You're often away, or busy or in another world, so to speak.

Tom A copywriter. Courtesy of 'Patient Aftercare'. Because, before I was admitted into the institution to become friends with my manic-depressive self, I first had to go into a clinic and get clean.
    'A versatile easy-to-maintain suit: drip-dry wear.'
    It puts my life back on a straight line. Well, it already had a 'line'.
    So I'm in a rented room again. The apartment is up for sale. And yet I've still managed to run up debts one way or another . . .

Pieter You must have stuck a fortune up your nose.

Tom A temporary room. With a sink smack in the middle of the wall.

Pieter Yes. With hindsight I could see it coming.

Tom But now I'm back. And Jan hasn't forgotten me! So you and Jan see each other regularly. That's great.

Pieter He's staying here for a few days.

Tom No, no! How fantastic. How wonderful! Bring Maarten back and we could all be dancing again! Dancing . . . oh . . . dancing . . . God, it's been such a long time since I did that. I just lover to dance, losing myself completely. (*He does a couple of ska steps.*) Nobody was as good as us, eh, Pieter? We knocked everyone dead. Didn't we? Women and men.

Pieter Yes.

Tom The four of us together, we must have had something irresistible. A lust for life and . . . oh . . . daring and . . . well . . . virility. It's hard to believe that now. But we must really have been like that. The case!

Pieter Yes. The case. I do have a bit of a problem, but maybe it's not such a big problem after all.

Tom I want to hear everything about it, and I mean everything.

> *Tom goes and sits on the couch. He is extremely 'concentrated'. Pieter looks at his friend for a while, sitting there on the couch motionless with his eyes closed, and then he starts to tell him everything.*

Pieter For years everyone's been getting something out of the department's social-club kitty. But not me. Or would you rather have a drink now and do this some other time?

Tom Piet . . . if you'd known, then you would have come?

Pieter Yes. Of course. Of course I would have.

Tom Those two months in the nut-house, Pieter, I was hardly the perfect host.

Pieter No, but . . . we've known each other for more than twenty years! Of course I should.

Tom I was happiest when I was sitting there cutting my arm or somebody else's with something or other. I was quite angry, I think.

Pieter With someone . . . in particular?

Tom Chemistry. Bad chemistry. Between me and myself.

Tom closes his eyes and makes a gentle motion with his hand: 'Go ahead, tell me.' Pieter stares at his friend on the couch for a little while. For a moment he has to overcome something before he can start again.

Get on with it then. Go for it. Come on.

Pieter Well, everyone in the department pays ten euros a month into the social club and everything is paid out of that: birthdays, weddings, births, flowers if you're in hospital, condolence wreaths, Christmas box for the cleaners, and new filters for the air-conditioning system because two of my colleagues think they're asthmatic. (*He looks at Tom.*) And . . . did they tell you what it might be?

Tom Acute mania.

Pieter And, uh . . . now?

Tom Lithium. Solid as a rock. Go on.

Tom is still sitting there with his eyes closed, and says nothing further, so Pieter continues his story.

Pieter I only qualify for 'birthdays'. The rest don't apply.

No reaction from Tom.

But even when it's my birthday I don't get anything from the kitty.

Tom You're quite a coward really, aren't you?

Pieter Yes. How?

Tom You've been with the council for twenty-one years?

Pieter Twenty-one, twenty-two years this year.

Tom A holiday job! It was a holiday job, Pieter. Twenty-one years!

Pieter Well . . . yes . . . Is that . . . terrible?

Tom C'mon, it's not really what you spent five years studying art history for. Is it? To run the archive at the Department of Culture?

Pieter And Welfare and Greater Metropolitan Policy.

Tom You should have written a book about Willem de Kooning. That's what you should have done. That was what you wanted to do.

Pieter Well, apparently not.

Tom Do you know what I still remember? From all those nights you spent talking about him in your student digs? That Willem was able to do something that we never would be able to.

Pieter Wow . . . what insight I had.

Tom Because he was able to capture an emotional state so precisely in paint on canvas.

Pieter Go on.

Tom Because he had the gift . . . 'to make the intangible tangible'.

Pieter Intangible tangible – that's just student bullshit, isn't it?

Tom Great nights. Because you understood something that I didn't understand.

Pieter It was just the talk of an artist *manqué*.

Tom A great passion. A great flame. That's what you had.

Pieter I had . . . what?

Tom A lust for life.

Pieter We all had that then.

Tom Not me.

Pieter Yes, you too. You most of all. You flung yourself into everything. You leapt into the canal. You swung from the chandelier. You rode a motorbike. I always held back.

Tom From art history to psychology to law. And it was all bollocks to me. Actually, I was already adrift then, don't you think? And I didn't give a toss about any of it. And you think: it'll all come when I start to practise . . . well . . . everything came when I was in practice, but not that great flame. No, no great flame. A great panic. More like. Go on. The case.

Pieter We'll ask someone else to handle the case.

Tom No! I want it. I want this. Come on. The case!

Pieter Well . . . that first year . . . when my holiday job was made permanent . . . the department kitty was already there.

Tom Department kitty? Oh . . . the department kitty. I thought you meant a cute secretary for a second. Sorry. Yes . . . the department kitty.

Pieter That first year, when the department realised they'd forgotten my birthday, I said . . . 'Don't worry about it. I don't want a present from the kitty.'

Tom Do you let people slap you around sometimes? Do you like that? You find that exciting, don't you? Sorry. Sorry, I'm listening.

Pieter I said: 'Well, to be honest, I'd rather have something out of the art depository.'

Tom The art depository?

Pieter That's the room underneath the city hall where all the public art is stored that has been more or less written off or unwanted.

Tom Why?

Pieter Why what?

Tom Why unwanted?

Pieter Not every gift the city council gratefully receives from our twin city is a joy to behold, Tom.

Tom That's what hospital walls are for, isn't it? If you knew what crap I've been looking at during my period in the nut-house.

Pieter There is crap, Tom, and there is *really* crap. *Really* crap we keep in the depository so it won't hurt anyone. It's the only storage facility that has water pipes running through it, and everybody just keeps on hoping for a bad leak that would remove the problem, literally and figuratively, but it's never happened.

Tom So on your birthday you were allowed to choose a piece of worthless art by your colleagues. Nice people, civil servants.

Pieter Four hundred square metres full of leftovers from the annual art festival, paintings dumped by the bailiffs. And stuff from the art school that no one else wants.

Tom Why not?

Pieter Because it is rubbish. Four hundred square metres of ugliness. It's a terrible thing, Tom, after a while it's effect is almost physical. The first few times I went downstairs, I don't know, I'd never experienced anything like it, not even in those horrible gay bars, but, after a quarter of an hour down there, I'd get appalling wind. Really, really terrible wind. I think it's a kind of defence mechanism. Do you understand?

Tom Defence – that's something I understand very little about. So, for twenty-one years, to celebrate your birthday, those officers of culture, welfare and greater metropolitan policy have allowed you to go down into the art depository, let off a couple of rancid farts, and pick out a piece of mouldy, sour, repulsive art.

Pieter I'd hand out the cakes and get an hour off.

Tom I don't think I'd like to go on holiday with your colleagues, but the case is quite clear to me. It's actually very simple, Piet. This sort of social-club kitty is like a collective insurance policy. You pay in an equal and pre-determined sum in fixed terms and in exchange for that you are insured with material effect on those couple of occasions in your life when it is thought you will have need of it. In your case we are talking about something on your birthday and a wreath on your coffin if you were to go the way of all flesh. You have paid your contribution dutifully every month for twenty-one years, and in exchange for that you should have received a respectable amount from the kitty on twenty-one separate occasions. This, madam judge, did not take place, I therefore propose that my client have the contributions paid in over the last twenty-one years returned to him in full. This amounts to a sum of, let's say, twenty-five hundred euros. We hope to see this sum returned forthwith. Thank you kindly. You have a good chance, Piet. And if the prosecution argues that you expressed a preference for payment of another sort, then they're not playing by the rules, and they can stick the flip-flap art from the cellar up their arses.

Pieter That isn't what I want. That is precisely what I don't want to happen. I want to keep it all. At least the eight Van Goppel paintings.

Jan is standing in the doorway. Tired.

Jan Tom.

Tom Jan. Jesus, Jan!

Tom wants to stand up but Pieter tugs at his sleeve.

Pieter They actually want the gifts back, Tom. The council wants them back, and I'm not going to give them back.

Tom What do you mean, back? They want to have that rubbish from the depository back? Jan . . . everything okay?

Tom and Jan embrace each other.

Jan I haven't forgotten you. Good to see you. Good to see you again! Everything swept back under the carpet? I sent you a card, and later flowers . . . I was sure you wouldn't have any use for a visitor. Otherwise I'd have come, naturally . . . I wrote on the card to let me know if you wanted me to come, and when I didn't hear anything I thought, he's right. Some things you have to do on your own.

Tom Yes.

Pieter How come you knew about this and I didn't? How come . . . Jan? He'd gone crazy! Why didn't you tell me!

Jan Not really crazy, surely. More overworked, right? Everyone could see it coming, couldn't they? I saw it coming, actually. But now everything's okay again?

Pieter He was walking through Barcelona in his under-pants, and he let himself be beaten up because it was in the script. I'd say that's a little bit more than overworked.

Jan Oh really, Tom?

Tom Shall I tell you about it?

Jan Yes, but you're here for the case.

Tom The case?

Jan Piet's. Piet's case.

Tom Yes, the case.

Pieter What exactly could you see coming, Jan?

Jan Well . . . it was obvious, workaholic, obsessive nature, the snorting . . . Something like this was bound to happen. But now everything's okay again?

Pieter Oh, yes.

Tom You want to keep it then, that rubbish?

Pieter It isn't rubbish! It isn't rubbish!

Jan takes a six-pack of beer out of a plastic bag from the night shop.

I'm very good. Maybe it's that flame, Tom . . . I'm good. I always have been. In a busy café I'm able to pick out the one. I can. On a crowded beach, at a dance . . . it doesn't make any difference . . . in a shopping centre . . . I pick out the one. I have an unsullied sensibility . . . a talent, say, for the real. For the untainted.

Jan Jesus, guys . . . just a second, Piet . . . there's something I need to get off my chest. (*And he sighs very deeply and despairingly. He opens a can on the couch.*) Sorry, but I've just come from home. Sorry. Won't take a second. I went home to pick up the mail. I come in. She's switched a lamp from the front room with a lamp from our bedroom! Why? Why? What is the point? What sort of craven act of defiance is that? There's a lamp from the bedroom by the couch. So I'm supposed to sit and read my post like this. (*He holds the aforementioned post up close to his eyes.*)

Pieter An uncompromising person. Someone who is! That's what I see. Something that is something. That's what I see. That speaks to me. In the cellar, where the ugliness is almost unendurable, I can see what's beautiful. Van Goppel.

Tom What? Who?

Pieter Van Goppel, Tom. They never gave him an exhibition; now he's dead. Now you can't even buy a screen print of his for less than ten thousand euros. In 1989 Van Goppel wasn't even able to pay his rent to the council. They had the nerve to charge him rent for that leaking dump of a place. And my esteemed colleagues actually sent in the bailiffs. Can you believe they really did that, Tom? Took everything he owned? His paint, his paintings, his everything? The last years of his life he lived and worked in a shed!

Jan There was a note lying on the table: 'Get some chips and something nice to go with them, I've gone to my salsa lesson. Mum.' She's taken up salsa. Conny hates that hip-swaying. She can't do it at all. She can't sway and she doesn't have any hips. Pure provocation.

Tom Do you have a girlfriend?

Jan Yes.

Pieter Oh yes?

Jan A girlfriend-ish woman, yes.

Pieter Oh yes? Oh yes? Then go and stay with her, Jan.

Jan I can't.

Pieter Why ever not.

Jan Because I think her husband might object.

Pieter Well . . . that's wonderful.

Tom Piet . . . one question . . . Why didn't you simply buy them? The paintings. Why didn't you buy them from the painter?

Pieter Tom . . . I paid for eight of his works . . . I saved them from the dump . . . I paid for them with my life! Forty hours a week, forty-eight weeks a year, twenty-one long years . . . I paid for them by working more than forty thousand hours. Do you understand what I'm saying? Everything . . . their total indifference to everything that they are not able to pigeon-hole . . . that bourgeois stupidity that they are so proud of . . . I've only been able to endure that for the last twenty-one years because I was allowed go down there once a year. If I have to give everything back now . . . well then . . . for those twenty-one years . . . I've let myself be ignored and humiliated for nothing. That can't be right, Tom. I couldn't cope with it. I couldn't live with it. I mean that. That is something I just couldn't live with.

Tom No. That's something that no one could live with.

Pieter Do you understand what's going on? Van Goppel is now worth a lot of money because of the Dokumenta festival, because of his death . . . now he finally gets an exhibition from the council. So they want to have everything back.

Tom Why are you so attached to them?

Pieter Because they're wonderful! Better than Willem de Kooning.

Tom Better than Willem?

Pieter Everyone saw him as a wannabe, a fake De Kooning, but I could see that that wasn't true. He was the same age as De Kooning and painted in the same style . . . and he was doing that from the very beginning, without . . . having seen his work, because Willem was already in New York. Tjebbo Van Goppel was an artist but he looked more like a greengrocer. He never left his home town. De Kooning was part of an exclusive coterie, a wonderful extremely attractive man, who was able to defend his own work eloquently and convincingly. But Van Goppel wasn't. He lived in self-imposed isolation. Van Goppel was better than De Kooning.

Jan He should have got himself an agent.

Pieter Who?

Jan That greengrocer you're on about. He should have been dragged out of that shed. Then he would have made it.

Pieter Jan, don't talk bullshit about things that you don't understand.

Tom You can't make it if you're not in the right place at the right time.

Pieter If you want to talk to me about art, say what you like, but please confine yourself to art. If you talk about the recession, I don't start prattling on about the visual appeal of the euro.

Tom How many of those paintings did you say you managed to dredge out of the council dump?

Pieter Eight. Are you listening?

Jan She comes downstairs, Teddy, and she says: 'Daddy, he's so sweet!' I run upstairs like a madman and what do you think I see lying there: a Berner Sennen! She's given the kids a dog! I say to Teddy – no idea where the other three are – I say: 'A lot has happened since Daddy's been away.' She says: 'Have you been away, then?' Isn't that awful? Conny is able to twist it so that my own children don't even miss me! I've been here almost a week! 'Have you been away, then?' I'm sorry, Tom, but I've just left home.

Tom Listen . . . just to play devil's advocate for a moment . . . if I was the council I'd have lodged a complaint against you.

Pieter What do you mean?

Tom For misappropriation.

Pieter Misappropriation?

Tom And that is, of course, what they'll do.

Pieter But you aren't the devil's advocate. You're my advocate.

Jan Misappropriation? I really can't have that, Piet. I'll be in the cabinet in a week.

Pieter They were given to me! Everyone knew about it. Even the head of department for cultural services, Vermeulen. He was saying: 'Happy birthday, Pieter, and please help yourself from the depository.' Are you really up to it, Tom? Is your brain sharp enough?

Perhaps they now look at the strange, tasteful art objects spread here and there throughout the room.

Tom Look . . . we'll have to get it in black and white from the council that they were really given to you as gifts.

Jan Yes, we will. Because a homosexual might just be acceptable, but a misappropriating homosexual, no way. I, um . . . shall I see what I can do?

Tom That would really make a difference, yes.

Pieter looks at Jan. For the first time there is a glimmer of hope.

Jan I'm going to, aren't I? I'm going to help. Aren't I?

Pieter What more could I expect?

Jan I'll get right onto it first thing.

Pieter But what can you actually do?

Jan I can have a word in the right ear.

Pieter But what can you actually do?

Jan I'll ask some questions. I'll need the names of the civil servants above you.

Pieter That already sounds a bit dodgy. Couldn't you just . . .

Jan Leave it to me. I know how these things work.

Tom How much are eight Van Goppels worth?

Pieter Of this . . . this quality . . . not lithos but canvases . . . somewhere between two and three million.

Tom and Jan stare at each other.

Tom You'll have to tell me the whole story again, Pieter, but now very slowly. Three million? Euros?

Jan Three million? For a couple of paintings? And where are they now?

Pieter I can't afford to have them hanging any longer. I could at first, but now that Van Goppel is dead . . . I can't pay the insurance any more. So they're in a safe.

Jan Three million?

Pieter You can sort this, Jan?

Jan Tom?

Tom Look, Piet, you could get away with buying New York for a couple of mirrors, you could get away with calling plastic 'imitation leather', you could even get away with calling an ugly-as-sin chipboard coffee table a wonderful example of craftsmanship, in a characteristic antique finish. You could get away with all these things – it wouldn't be right . . . but you could get away with them all. But in your case, if nobody confirms that you really received those paintings as gifts, then you're fucked!

Pieter So we have to make sure that someone comes forward. Right, Jan?

Jan Jesus fucking Christ, Pieter, you're going to have to help me. I need every defect . . . every stain . . . every failure, every omission, every mistake . . . I need a valuation error . . . a deficit, a smear . . . a blunder . . . and I need it badly. Three million. There've been ministers who've had to resign for less. I can't do this myself, I'll have to put someone on to it. Jesus, this is all I need.

Pieter Yes, I'm pretty chuffed about it myself.

Jan If it comes down to it, settle, I'd say. What about you, Tom?

Tom Yeah . . . but it seems like a good idea first to check if there's anything unsavoury going around about Vermeulen.

Jan That's something you can help with too.

Pieter Is there really no better way?

Jan Something perverse, improper, scandalous, too much booze, can't keep his hands to himself, fingers in the till, anything that can't be covered up, every row, every indiscretion. Something with blood on it, do you understand? I need something that requires a little compensating.

Pieter But does it have to be like that? Can't it be less vulgar?

Jan You do want to keep those bloody things?

And there is Maarten standing in the doorway.
Holding the same plastic bag from the night shop.

Maarten Lads! Lads! All three of you! Cloaca! I've just come from rehearsals, or more precisely from your house, Jan, to drop off Laura, and heard the news that you'd left. Nice dog. Thunder. Isn't he! Tom here too. I heard that you were a little mixed up for a while. It's terrible that something like that can happen to you without your friends realising it.

Pieter Except for the fact that you realised it!

Maarten You were in some sort of health spa for a while, I heard.

Pieter Health spa? He was cutting his arm with a shard of glass.

Maarten No! I've only known about it for a couple of days! Someone told me. I said: 'That can't be true. Tom is a friend of mine, I'd know about it,' but well, we've often not seen each other for a while, and I've got a new play coming up. Lads . . . it's a wonderful play! And it's four hours again, so no moaning about it being half a day's work. So you were up on a roof in a Batman cape?

Tom I only know about the underpants in Barcelona.

Maarten Then all that talk about the Batman cape is probably exaggerated.

Tom I hope so.

Pieter I don't think so.

Maarten embraces Tom warmly.

Maarten But . . . you seem better now. No longer nuts.

Tom De-nutsed.

Maarten Good! Very good! You'll have to tell me all about it.

Tom Now?

Maarten passes out beers. Points to all four men and does a ska dance from the old days.

Maarten Do you know, I've been thinking about this quite a lot lately. We were good, weren't we? Why don't we recycle ourselves? Shocking Blue are performing again. Seriously. Do you fancy that? Performing at eighties parties?

Jan Well . . . let's just wait for the announcement of the cabinet first.

Maarten Jan. She's good!

Jan Who?

Maarten Laura. Your Laura. I always take her home, it's on my way, and tonight she said: 'Come in and have a look at Thunder.'

Jan That Berner Sennen?

Maarten Nice animal, Jan. So?

Jan So? What do you mean, so? What are you getting at?

Pieter This time I'm not going to be the referee because I've got a problem of my own.

Maarten (*to Pieter*) Oh? (*to Jan*) The cabinet. Any news yet?

Jan No! Why are you taking Laura home?

Maarten Because it's right before the opening. We're rehearsing late into the early hours. I had no idea that things were so bad between you and Conny. Hey, it's so nice to see you guys again. Just like old times.

Pieter You aren't supposed to say that sort of thing, Maarten, you're only supposed to think it.

Jan With my Laura? Rehearsing?

Maarten Arranged months ago. You knew, didn't you? She could take part as long as I brought her home at night. Conny said she couldn't go down by the canal on her bike on her own.

Jan What's the name of it . . . this thing . . . what's it called?

Maarten *Wheel of Ixion.*

Jan *Wheel of Ixion*, yes. That's . . . that's what Laura's doing. *Wheel of Ixion*. Is it a play?

Pieter No, it's a game show.

Jan Yes, see, that's what I thought too.

Pieter *Wheel of Ixion*! Theatre! Pleb!

Jan Is it really a play?

Maarten Yes!

Jan I knew Laura was doing some sort of work experience with you, but I thought . . . *Wheel of Ixion* . . .

Maarten What?

Jan I actually thought that you were directing a game show. I thought Laura would be holding up cards in a pretty dress or giving the wheel a spin or something.

Maarten No. Come on, no. God, no, Jan. Come on! Surely by now you know what I make.

Jan So she has to act for you?

Pieter *Wheel of Ixion*, Jan, Greek mythology.

Jan How should I know, I studied economics!

Maarten We open in four days. It's really great to see you guys again. We've seen far too little of each other lately.

Pieter You could go mad and nobody notice.

Jan So my daughter is acting in a play for you?

Tom Yes, Jan. Your daughter is working with Maarten. What's your problem? It's a play. Not a peep-show.

Jan Oh no? You know his kind of theatre.

Maarten What do you mean by that?

Jan Exactly what I say.

Maarten I'm not going to take that from you, Jan. I'm not going to take it. What's your problem? What are you trying to say?

Jan Just what I am saying.

Maarten I'm an artist, and occasionally, for artistic reasons, someone might have to show their bare arse, yes, and if you think that's porn, well that's your problem.

Jan Does Laura have to show her bare arse, Maarten? Does my daughter have to show her bare arse for artistic reasons?

Maarten Your daughter specifically wanted to do her training with me. Everyone wants to do their training with me.

Jan Showing her bare arse?

Maarten I could have had any student, from any theatre school, to play her role, but I let Laura do it.

Jan Showing her bare arse, Maarten?

Maarten Because she really wanted to and because her father's my friend. But if you're saying that you don't want her to . . . then she's out.

Jan That isn't what I'm saying. That's what you are making of it, but that isn't what I'm saying at all.

Maarten Because if that's true I'll just drive back to your house right now and tell her she's out.

Jan Does she have to show her bare arse, Maarten?

Maarten Yes. For a moment. Yes.

Jan See. Am I right or am I right? Bare-arse time again.

Maarten Just tell me what you want, Jan. We've still got four days before the opening. Do I need to replace her?

Jan No, you have to put a dress on her.

Maarten Not possible. I can't do that for artistic reasons!

Jan Oh fuck off with your artistic reasons. You'd stick Snow White in a G-string and strap a three-foot cock on to all nine dwarfs for artistic reasons. Bullshit!

Pieter Seven.

Maarten You are just . . .

Jan No, I'm not a fan of your work and you've known that for a good long time. It has nothing to do with my daughter's bare arse, apart from the fact that we happen to be talking about it at the moment. But it has nothing to do with Laura's bare arse.

Tom Yes it has.

Pieter Yes it absolutely has.

Jan No no no no! I've been saying that for years. *We've* been saying that for years! Every time we see one of your performances we say: 'It's great that he can earn a living from this, but do we really have to have it inflicted on us twice a year?'

Pieter *You* say that?

Tom Yes, you always say that, yes you do.

Maarten What's wrong with you all of a sudden, Jan?

Tom Laura.

Jan Thank you, Tom! That's not it at all.

Maarten What?

Pieter Why are you here, Maarten? I want to go to bed. Jan has the guest room. Tom's sleeping on the couch, so . . . (*He gestures Maarten to leave.*)

Tom Oh?

Pieter You're not going back to that tiny gloomy room with the washbasin in the middle of the wall. Don't even think about it.

Tom Oh. Okay.

Maarten You want her out of the play? You want her to go, Jan?

Jan None of us gives a toss about what you do, right. And Tom certainly doesn't.

Maarten Is this all because Laura is naked for a second?

Jan No, it's because it's all true! Before we go to an opening of yours we all have four double espressos! That is twenty-four espressos in total, and after about three hours Tom still leans against Pieter and has a nap.

Pieter Which is no picnic at all for Pieter. But the espressos. It's just because I love espressos.

Maarten Is that right, Tom? Do you fall asleep in the theatre?

Tom Yes.

Maarten That hurts.

Tom Pieter always makes a point of wearing that checked suit with the thick shoulder-pads, and then it's okay for both of us.

Jan And we – (*emphasising*) – *we* think the worst thing is the music. You're sitting there having a nice nap and then that terrible music comes crashing in. It scares me to death every time. A dress! My daughter has to have a dress on!

Maarten You're jealous.

Jan What am I supposed to be jealous of? You haven't been fooling around with her, have you? With your filthy director's hands? Why did you go into my house?

Maarten To have a look at Thunder. She asked me to.

Jan Thunder. You get out of your car just to have a look at Thunder.

Maarten I thought you'd be home. Yes, Thunder. Because she only got him on Wednesday.

Jan Who?

Maarten Who? Laura. She was eighteen on Wednesday, wasn't she?

Jan is struck dumb, but doesn't twitch a muscle.

Jan I have to make a call, lads. (*He walks off.*)

Maarten It's not hard to remember, because her birthday's exactly one week before his. That's something I still remember.

Pieter Me too. And you, Tom?

Tom Yes. How old was he then? When Laura was born?

Pieter Twenty-six.

Tom Twenty-six. And Laura one week old. That was beautiful, wasn't it?

Pieter I've no idea what you mean.

Tom Yes you have.

Pieter Yes, well, yes, but we've heard that story often enough. I can see you're about to tell it again, but enough. Why do you always have to do that?

Tom Because it was so lovely.

Pieter That I cried.

Tom Yes. Do it again?

Pieter No.

Tom God, did you bawl, Pieter.

Pieter You see? This is what I mean. This is amusing you.

Tom No, not amusing. Lovely. Won't you do a bit again?

Pieter No.

Maarten Eighteen years. Insane, isn't it? Did I hold her then? Laura?

Tom Jan gave her to Piet first. Piet was very moved . . . He cried so hard that he was afraid he was going to drop her and then he passed her to you.

Maarten Insane.

Pieter That was really the high point of your life, wasn't it, eh? The fact that I cried.

Tom grips Pieter tightly.

37

Tom You won't suddenly flip. Maybe you won't be happy either, but you won't go mad. You can do it again. Have the feeling.

Pieter Don't talk such sentimental bollocks. It was only that . . . I saw Jan, our Jan . . . with that little person. And well . . . it was beautiful. Simply very, very beautiful. Have you ever seen him so happy since . . . well? Ever?

Maarten Yeah. God, did you cry, Pieter.

Pieter Yes, ha ha! Ha ha! I cried. Cried like a baby. Don't you think that it might also have had something to do with the fact that we thought a magnum of champagne wasn't such a suitable present for a birth and that we ended up drinking it before we went? Did it perhaps have something to do with the smell in that house . . . Conny with her hair down in bed, with no make-up and so sweet? That face of Conny's, like marzipan. That skin. So intensely white. Two litres of blood lost! But alive and back home with a daughter. With Jan so proud?

Tom The fact that he gave her away. To you. Laura. That's . . . when you broke down.

Pieter Yes, Tom, that's when I broke down.

Maarten God, I never realised how narrow-minded you are. Who'd believe it? Bloody hell.

Pieter Maarten . . . just go home. We all have to go to bed.

Maarten So you don't give a toss about what I make?

Tom We often ask why you don't do plays like you used to when you were a student.

Maarten Come on, those plays were so uncomplicated.

Tom Yes.

Pieter Yes.

Maarten You can't stand still. At some point it has to be for real!

Tom Says who?

Maarten Time moves on. You can't stand still. We don't greet each other with 'Cloaca' any more, do we! That's over.

Pieter When you came in just now you said it again.

Maarten For sentimental reasons. But Pieter . . . you, surely? You like my plays, don't you? Or . . . are you also suddenly . . .

Pieter Well, to be honest, lately I haven't given a shit about your plays. Now go home.

Maarten Well . . . that's just great. The fact that I've been working for twenty-odd fucking years trying to build something unique, a totally individual style, I've never played safe, never fallen into the trap of success, kept innovating, taken risks . . . I'm more famous abroad than I am here, but I'm still somebody here too, that can't have escaped you, and the only ones that think it's all been for nothing are my friends. Amazing.

Tom Maybe because we knew you when you were still a nobody. So now we keep thinking: cut the crap. Why all that screaming, and why is there always someone with a bare arse?

Pieter Maybe I'm a bit emotional in everybody's eyes. It's true that I feel a lot, but over the last few years, Maarten, I've felt less and less for your plays. I'm afraid that's the truth.

Maarten Are you going soft?

Pieter No, you're getting hard.

Maarten You should all get tickets for *Holiday on Ice* at Christmas. That'll be art enough for you.

Pieter Can I go to bed?

Maarten Does he have a girlfriend?

Pieter That's something we don't ask.

Maarten So he does have a girlfriend. I'm asking because otherwise you'll have Jan sitting here like the sulking birthday boy in three days.

Pieter In three days Jan will be back home with his family.

Maarten I wouldn't be so sure.

Pieter Oh. That's great . . . I'm not going to be stuck here on my own with sulking birthday boy Jan. You'll all have to come too, and we'll take him out to dinner or something.

Maarten I'm not coming, It's my opening night the next day.

Tom I think it's a bit lame, going out to dinner. He's going to be forty-three! I'm not going out to dinner with the three of you. Four middle-aged men out to dinner because it's someone's birthday. Depressing! I'm just getting back on my feet again. I don't want to go out to dinner, the four of us sat at a round table. That won't be any fun. You'll pick an expensive restaurant, where you can't let your hair down. It'll be boring. The whole evening I'll be thinking: another twenty years and then they'll bring it in. Meals on wheels . . . dinner in a tiny polystyrene box.

Pieter What are you on about now? What are you on about now? Do you want some pyjamas?

Tom Something fun! Something . . . exciting. Something . . . that'll make him feel again.

Pieter You way overestimate 'feeling', Tom. It isn't that great at all. And it's only his birthday. Dinner. That's it.

Maarten I can't come.

Tom Oh yes! Yes, you can!

Maarten Oh yes?

Tom starts to laugh out loud.

Tom What a great idea!

Darkness.

Pieter is just about to leave; he already has his coat on. Jan has just come in.

Pieter I have to go.

Jan You understand what this means, don't you?

Pieter Yes. Yes. Nice for you. But I have to go now.

Jan Wonderful. And to hear it today of all days.

Pieter Well, there you go.

Jan This interview, Pieter, it's just a formality. The moment that the whip invites you in for an interview it's already been decided. So it's already been decided. 'FO. It's going to be the FO. Who else could do the FO?

Pieter Great, isn't it?

Jan And that I should hear today.

Pieter I really have to go now.

Jan Because it's my birthday today, I mean.

Pieter Yes, I heard what you said. But I have to go. It wasn't my idea. Sorry.

Pieter exits, leaving Jan behind alone. He makes a call.

Jan Can you talk? (. . .) It's happening. I'm seeing the whip the day after tomorrow. In half an hour you and I will be driving to Maastricht or Ghent or Bruges, where ever you like, Jenny. Say you've got a rush job on, I'm taking you out for an expensive dinner, and we'll be sleeping at a thousand-euro-a-night hotel. Do you have time to change? Something sexy? (. . .) I think Foreign Affairs. I'm not a party ideologist. I'm not a standard-bearer. I'm a personality, and they know that. They have to give me room. They know that. Abroad, Jenny. Abroad a lot. Freedom . . . I can finally let everybody see what I am! (. . .) But it's my birthday, sweetheart, you haven't forgotten, have you? (. . .) Yes, Jesus, a ten-minute meeting . . . can't he do that? (. . .) Your husband! Oh no, Jenny, don't ruin the best night of my life because you have to go to a ten-minute meeting with a history teacher. (. . .) Tutor, same thing. (. . .) Oh, sweetheart, all children do strange things at that age. (. . .) Didn't you ever skip school? (. . .) Stoned in class . . . How would a teacher know that anyway, did she carry out a urine test on your son? They are just talking crap, honestly . . . (. . .) Yes. (. . .) Yes. (. . .) Yes. (. . .) Yes. (. . .) Sorry. Goodbye, sweetheart. Have a nice ten-minute meeting (. . .) Yes. 'Bye, sweetheart. (*He stares vacantly into space. Then he calls again.*) This is Daddy. Is Mummy home? (. . .) Call her, Bram. (. . .)

Meanwhile four male ska dancers have appeared behind him. In very short checked trousers, very large suit jackets, beneath them white T-shirts, sunglasses, trilbies, three-quarter-length raincoats.

What do you mean, she can't come to the phone! Just tell her that it's very important. She has to come! (. . .) Bram . . . it doesn't interest Daddy one iota if Mummy is busy cooking Spanish in the kitchen and I don't give a

fuck if Mummy says that it'll all burn; she has to come
to the phone. Now! Now, Bram. Tell Mummy that she
has to come to the telephone! Conny! (*He screams out
his anger.*) Conny, come to the phone immediately!
Conny!

> *Then one of the ska men turns on a ghetto-blaster. It's
> 'Madness' or some such. They perform a ska dance in
> formation. They look amusing and energetic. Jan does
> not understand what's happening to him. As they
> dance they get closer and closer to him. When they are
> right by him he becomes involved in the dance because
> one or another of them keeps touching him. As the
> dance continues, their touches become increasingly
> cheeky and erotic. It's all something of a surprise for
> Jan, who is buffeted back and forth between extremely
> positive and extremely negative emotions. Jan tries to
> discover who is who, and also what the identity of the
> fourth ska dancer is. He is drawn into the front of the
> line, and as they make the sideways ska movement, it's
> just as if Jan is being 'ridden'. Champagne is laid ready
> and two glasses. The lights are dimmed. Then the four
> ska dancers leave as suddenly as they appeared. Jan
> has to make an effort to recover. Then someone calls.*

Yes?

> *He looks towards the door, or opens it. A ska man is
> standing there with a ghetto-blaster. The man comes
> in, turns on the ghetto-blaster. It now plays sexy strip
> music. Prince? Once again Jan is totally dumbfounded.
> The 'man' sits him down gently in the middle of the
> couch and a professional strip act follows. The fourth
> ska man turns out to be a woman, who has sexy
> lingerie under the ska outfit, which she wears in an
> aggressive style; latex suspenders and thigh-high boots.
> When Jan realises what is intended, any question
> of hesitation is soon dispelled and he submits to it*

all with delight. The lady is a professional. She
unashamedly flings her legs up right before Jan's eyes.
She turns her arse towards him and he understands
that he can peel off her panties. She pulls him to the
floor and performs every sort of suggestive and
exciting act with him that can be imagined, without
losing command over the situation. Jan is really getting
wound up. Beneath the panties it turns out there is a
mini feathered G-string. She continues to dance right.
in front of him wearing this. Meanwhile she has
popped the cork from a bottle of champagne and
pours it all over them both. Jan is encouraged to lick
it off, from her breasts to her G-string. This he does
eagerly. Until his tongue encounters something strange
beneath the small, feathered G-string. It distracts him,
and he wants to dispel it from his mind, but the damage
has been done. His tongue again feels something
strange beneath the G-string. He leads her into the
light. What he sees immediately strips him of all his
desire. The Call Girl does her best to get him going
again, but Jan just stands there, angry and uninterested.
She then gives up and goes and sits on the couch, not
even offended, and drinks a glass of champagne.

Sorry, but if you do something like this it has to be
perfect. Perfect. Sorry. Maybe I'm a bit inflexible about
this . . . but this kind of gift can be tricky. You
understand that, don't you? If someone does something
like this, they have to do it one hundred per cent right.
I think it's a fantastic gesture by the lads, though . . . (*He*
checks the brand of champagne.) Did you bring this with
you? It's from your firm, I suppose. All included, I'm
sure. This is how they make their profit, with this sort
of rot-gut. Have a cigarette, take one of those. Make
yourself comfortable. I'm not offended. You are, uh . . .
good. Really good . . . but . . . I'm turning forty-five,
I've just left home, I've been waiting two months for

some news . . . some important news . . . from my employer . . . and now it's come . . . my girlfriend can't be with me because she has to have a ten-minute meeting this evening, yesterday she couldn't get away because someone was calling round with upholstery samples for the couch . . . and the day before yesterday she pulled a muscle jogging. That's when you know, don't you? Well, I know all right. It was a lovely idea from the lads . . . a really lovely idea . . . with the ska music as well . . . and I'd no idea who the fourth dancer was . . . They'd really thought about it . . . and paid . . . and rehearsed that dancing with you . . . really nice . . . (*He grows a little emotional.*) What a really good idea of theirs. You. And good too. I've got to admit it. You are really good.

He goes and sits next to her on the couch. Thinks that he can touch her anywhere. Fondles her breasts a little. Wants to kiss her, seeing as it's already been paid for, but she is able to avoid it. She starts to perform again. Stands and turns with her arse to his face, whilst gazing vacantly into the auditorium. He sinks from the couch to his knees and then peels down her thigh-high boots, as far as possible. He sits on his knees as she turns towards him. His face is right up close to the G-string.

Sorry. (*He walks to the other side of the room, doesn't know what to do with himself, and starts to cry.*) It has to be perfect, do you understand? (*He points to the border of her G-string.*) It has to be different to this. And normally it wouldn't be a problem, but not at the moment! Not at the moment!

She looks at her G-string.

That . . . that's a Caesarean scar. You've got a scar there from a Caesarean. And . . . I can cope with just about anything . . . wrinkles, pot belly . . . bad teeth . . . I'm

really, uh . . . not that squeamish . . . but . . . that scar . . .
you understand . . . that scar . . . now, right now . . . it
just makes me limp. Sorry. You know you can go if you
want. It's all right by me if you leave. Or . . . wait a minute.
It would be better for the lads if . . . we could both take a
nap and then you can bugger off after an hour or so. I'll
tell them some hot story . . . everyone'll be happy.

*He goes and sits next to her, pats her amicably on the
thigh. Then stares straight ahead for a while.*

And yes . . . when I think about it now: where and when
and why did I let it all slip through my fingers? When
did Conny and I stop loving each other, I wonder? That
mark . . . that scar . . . that um . . . hit a nerve. I think
I've only ever seen something like that on my wife's belly.
Never on someone else's body, definitely not when I was
um . . . about to . . . as I said . . . pot belly, wrinkles . . .
oh . . . once I even discovered an enormous gash on a
woman who was missing a kneecap; it kind of . . . had
something . . . but . . . this . . . you understand? This is
my story. (*He cries.*) Conny had been in labour for thirty-
two hours! I put her in the bath, we stood under the
shower, then in the bath again, under the shower, in the
bath, back to bed . . . thirty-two hours. The midwife said:
'What a super-team the two of you are.' But the baby just
wouldn't come. It didn't come. And Conny was in pain.
And no baby. No baby. Dilated eight centimetres. No
baby. After thirty-six hours she couldn't speak any longer.
Conny. She kept hold of my hand, though. She wouldn't
let me go. Not even . . . to the toilet. But she couldn't
speak, wasn't speaking any more. She didn't want to go
on. I thought: 'She's going to die.' I thought: 'This is not
going to be the birth of my first child, this is going to be
the death of my wife.' God knows, I just didn't know
what to do. What can you do! No more candles, no tea,
no warm bath . . . all bullshit. Then the midwife said:

46

'she can't go on, we're going to the hospital.' I heard her calling an ambulance. I thought: everything is over. We're going to lose Conny. I'm going to lose Conny.

Then . . . I can't remember the details now . . . the ambulance . . . hospital . . . Conny gets a drip in her hand full of oxytocin. She lying there, me bending over her, with her head in my hands, and while I keep an eye on the contractions on one monitor, and on the babies heartbeat on the other, I say to her: 'It's going to be all right. It's all going to be all right.' And I think: 'Oh God, don't let her die. If you just won't let her die, I'll take anything else you deal out. We'll have a new baby, there'll be some grief, but don't let Conny die.' And so we sit there. And we wait. And then suddenly she says something. I can't understand her. She looks at me and says: 'We're going to push.' And I think: 'It's going to be okay, everything will be okay.' Conny pushes. And I thank the God that I don't believe in, but I did at that moment. And then another push. And another. But suddenly I could tell by the people around us that there was something wrong. I could hear, before I understood, that the beat of the CTG had changed. I just knew something was wrong. The beat of the heart. Had changed. Slower . . . a lot, lot slower. Then . . . I find myself running in the midst of people rushing through a corridor. Someone hurls me into green overalls, someone leads me to a tap, someone says I have to wash my hands, I get a mask, a hat, paper slippers over my shoes. Someone says 'umbilical cord' and 'Caesarean'. Someone takes me to the operating room where Conny is lying. Out. Total narcosis. Someone hands me a camera and says: 'Take a lot of photos, take a lot of photos.' And I do. With someone to my left and someone to my right ready to catch me if I faint and to stop me getting too close because that could infect the incision in her belly. Which I only understood later. Much later. I click and click and click, and I think,

how clever of them, to give me something to do. Later
I hear that it was really necessary to take the photos.
To convince Conny that the baby in her arms was really
hers. Do you understand. A lot of women who give birth
under narcosis have doubts for the rest of their lives.
I didn't know about that. We don't feel like that. We
never know for sure, but we never have any doubts either.
If we had been ten minutes later, little Laura would have
strangled herself. She was getting herself born, whilst
with every contraction she was being strangled tighter
and tighter by the umbilical cord. Around her neck. It
turned out it was around her neck. Premature suicide,
it's been called. But she did get born. 'A super-team.'
(*He has to cry.*) Sorry. I'm sure you haven't seen anything
like this before. A man crying his eyes out. Or have you?
And do you know who were always there for me? Do
you know who knew how I felt? The lads. Who are now
shivering their arses off outside somewhere. Why is it
that everything has got worse?

*He goes and sits next to her on the couch. The Call
Girl is nice to him. Puts an arm around him. She also
starts to talk now, but in Russian. Jan doesn't
understand a word of it, but it is also an emotional
story, he can tell that by looking at her. In some way
or other it consoles him. While she is talking in her
low, melancholy voice, he lays his head in her lap and
she strokes his hair. The crying fit has tired him out.
He feels very 'cleansed'.*

Call Girl (*Russian*) If you could understand me, we
might really have a nice time together, man with no
name. I sense so much sadness in you. But what's wrong?
Is your wife dead? Oh, I hope for your sake that she isn't.
Something to do with this scar on my belly, eh? I had a
weird feeling about tonight. Nobody notices this scar,
sweetheart. They're all blind horny. Nobody's ever paid

any attention to it. You are the first. And then you go and cry. Oh . . . who knows . . . maybe you could really be a good man for me. I bear a lot of sadness too, sweetheart. A lot of sadness. I'm not a whore, you know, I'm a mother. But one from a rotten country. Don't you think I'd rather be with my daughters? Of course. Every mother wants to be with her child. But it isn't possible.

Maarten, Tom and Pieter slip into the apartment and are quite surprised by the scene unfolding on the couch.

Call Girl (*Russian*) What do you think? That I'm going to let all these fellers have me for the price of an expensive pair of shoes? No, my daughters. Of course, my two daughters! They board at an exclusive international school. My children are never cold, never hungry, will never let themselves be hit by a man. They'll say: 'Piss off, arsehole, I've got no use for you.' Because they're going to study. They can be whatever they want. Doctors. Lawyers . . . I'll let myself be squeezed blue and fucked raw for my darling children. Just three more years. Do you understand? Just three more years. Then I can go home, and everything will be fine.

She vacantly strokes Jan's hair and face. He is completely disarmed. He strokes her. Maarten, Tom and Pieter had expected something quite different.

Jan We understand each other rather well, eh? Yes, we understand each other. Now don't be alarmed if I start crying again. Only for a bit. There's still something inside of me. A sort of old storm, which just won't blow over. A rain cloud that's been hanging over me for years. Can't it just rain empty? It's strange that you can suddenly feel it like this. I know exactly where it is, it's here at the back of my head. And it's been there a long, long time and I want to be rid of it. (*He sighs deeply a couple of times.*) Oh God . . . oh God . . . oh God . . .

The girl strokes him and sings a Russian lullaby. Jan
continues sobbing. Maarten, Tom and Pieter can't
believe their eyes. Without Jan's noticing, Maarten taps
the Call Girl on the shoulder. Gestures: 'Have you had
a fuck?' She continues singing while gesturing no. The
lads don't know what to do. They want to go, but the
Call Girl signals: 'I'm leaving in ten minutes, who's
going to pay me?' Oh yes, the envelope. Tom gives
the envelope to the Call Girl, and while she is stroking
the weeping Jan and singing a Russian lullaby, she
gestures: 'Let me see, what's inside, count it out where
I can see it.' Tom takes out the money and they count
it together. Some three hundred euros. In the meantime,
Jan has noticed there is something going on and he
opens his eyes. From the corner of his eye he sees the
account being settled. The girl is just signing the
receipt at Tom's request. Jan sits up straight.

Jan Hey . . . shut it for a minute with all that sentimental
Russian twaddle. What a surprise, lads. What a surprise!

Maarten We were freezing our nuts off outside.

Jan Yes, of course, course.

Maarten We thought: he's having a fuck in the bedroom.

Jan Yes . . . sure . . .

Maarten We thought: we'll slip in and have a quiet beer.

Jan Oh yeah. Yeah.

Maarten Hadn't occurred to us that you might fuck her
in the here and now.

Pieter I didn't think it was a very good idea. I said so,
didn't I? It wasn't a good idea. He's not in the right state
of mind for it.

Maarten He doesn't have to be in the right state of mind,
Piet.

Jan It went a little differently . . . but . . . wonderful.

Tom Didn't you two fuck?

Jan Nope.

Maarten What . . . no!

Tom What difference does it make! What difference does it make! Fucking can be a very depressing experience, Maarten, maybe this was a little more interesting.

Maarten That's not what we paid a hundred euros each for! For her to run her fingers through his hair a bit and snivel out some song. Fuck it, I'd do that for nothing.

Tom It doesn't make any difference! It's fine! It's fine like this!

Maarten What! Three hundred euros! This isn't third-world aid, guys, it's business. She's been sitting on her arse all this time; it's an easy night for her as it is. For three hundred euros, she can do a little dance for us now. Come and sit down here, Piet, have a butcher's at a tasty bit of flesh for a change.

Jan She can go home.

Maarten No way. There is no way she's going home. You! Dance!

Jan Maarten . . .

Maarten I've got my opening night tomorrow, Jan, can't I just enjoy a bit of R&R?

Call Girl (*Russian*) Are you trying to order me about, mister?

Maarten Dance. Do your job!

The Call Girl walks over to him and strokes his face.

Call Girl (*Russian*) Ask nicely, you son of a bitch. Ask very, very nicely.

Maarten Just dance, five minutes. That's all.

Call Girl (*Russian*) Elena's the name, please.

Maarten Fucking bitch.

Call Girl (*Russian*) Elena's the name, please.

Maarten What does she want now?

Tom It's odd, but I think she wants you to treat her like a human being.

Maarten You mean she wants me to say please? Is this some kind of S&M thing? Is she going to beat me up if I don't?

Tom She might not, but I will. Behave, Maarten. (*He turns on the television, and sits on the couch flipping channels.*)

Pieter Hey, whose house is this, anyway?

Tom It could have been really lovely.

Jan It was, Tom. (*Jan goes and sits beside him on the couch.*) Truly. Thank you. Was it your idea? You madman.

> They watch television and both laugh a little. Tom gestures: 'Lay your head in my lap.'

No.

Tom You liked it, didn't you?

Jan No.

Pieter Yes! And now everyone go home!

Jan But I'm staying here.

Pieter Go to your room then.

Tom And I'm crashing here because I can't be left on my own.

Jan stretches out on the couch with his head in Tom's lap.

Pieter My dear Elena, thank you for this lovely evening. Will you please leave us alone now?

Maarten She was going to dance!

Pieter This is my house, my life . . . you're a son of a bitch and that woman can go home. What's wrong with you! Being a bit horny's okay, but what you're doing is just embarrassing.

Maarten Come on! It doesn't do anything for you because of your dippy poofter dick, but I'll tell you this, that is a boy's dream.

Pieter Dippy poofter dick?

Jan It's my present and I say she can go home.

Maarten Then I'm going to take her into the bedroom for a little while. Paid is paid, boys.

Pieter There's no way you're going into my bedroom.

Maarten What's wrong with you? What's wrong with you all of a sudden? Just because I call you a dippy poofter dick? It doesn't mean a thing. It doesn't bother me at all. Never has. Do you think I've been your friend for more than twenty years just to make something of that now? Bugger off. (*Maarten walks towards Pieter, hugs him firmly and kisses him full on the mouth.*) Does it bother me? It doesn't bother me at all. You know that, don't you?

Pieter is totally nonplussed by this unwanted intimacy. Tom motions: 'Come and sit here.' Pieter goes and sits next to Tom, who puts an arm around him. Maarten realises that he has gone too far.

Guys! Let me have a bit of fun. I've got the opening tomorrow.

Maarten is the only one standing now, the rest are sitting on the couch. Helena moves towards him. Seductively dancing a little. She touches him here and there. Whispers something in his ear. Stands behind him and lets her hands slide downwards from his shoulders. Extremely sensually. Maarten sees his dream coming true. The other three are watching television. Then, just as Helena's hands approach his crotch she performs a little mime: her hands first search carefully for his cock, but she soon signals to the other three: 'What's this?' She searches more frantically, 'forgets' her sensual play-acting. Searches feverishly and finally removes her hands from his trousers.

Call Girl You are a tiny little man.

Then she goes. Maarten is deeply offended. The other three act as if they haven't seen anything. We can hear that they are watching football.

Maarten Lads. This would make a horse jealous.

Jan Maarten . . . break a leg.

Maarten You guys don't have to come tomorrow.

Jan Will my daughter have a dress on?

Maarten As far as I'm concerned none of you have to come. Conny's coming. And you wouldn't want to deal with that, would you, Jan? Her in row one and you in row fourteen.

Jan Will my daughter have a dress on?

Maarten You can come some other day. You're not that crazy about opening nights, as you've just told me.

Jan Will my daughter have a dress on?

Maarten Nobody! Nobody! No management, no administrator, no producer, no critic is ever going to tell

54

me how I should do a play. I never compromise my art for anyone.

Jan So?

Maarten Not for emotional blackmail either.

Everyone knows what he means, but nobody has the energy to take up the point. It is clear that everyone wants Maarten to leave and he feels it.

I get the impression . . . one way or another . . . that since you've all been living here I've become the fall guy. I'm the same person I've always been. But I don't seem to be able to do anything right. First of all, you think my work is total shit and now you think I'm not treating that woman properly. She doesn't have any problem with it. Only you. I'm still the same. If there's anyone here who has done exactly what he wanted to all his life, done what he *had* to do, then it's me. I've always done what I've wanted to and without compromise. None of you can say that. Look at yourselves. Just look at yourselves for a moment. From here it's a pretty pathetic sight, the three of you.

Tom 'Romantic covers-sets with a flowery motif at a super price.'

Maarten Sorry?

Tom 'An attractive brassiere with soft moulded cups, which create a beautiful plunging neckline. Wonderful comfort and the best in modern contouring.'

Maarten I . . . what? Just admit it. Admit it. All three of you are jealous of me.

Tom 'A blazer with a large woven mink-styled fur collar. Modestly trimmed at the waist. With a finished hem and highly attractive cuffs.'

Maarten has no idea what to make of these oracle-like statements.

Maarten More beer, everyone?

Pieter There is no more beer.

Maarten Shall I get some?

All three nod. Maarten checks his pockets to see if he has any money and goes out. Tom is still sitting with his arm around Pieter, who does not find this at all unpleasant, and Jan is still lying with his head in Tom's lap.

Tom I've been thinking, Piet . . . you can find something beautiful in the middle of so much ugliness, right?

Pieter Yes.

Tom Only things, or people too?

Pieter People too.

Tom Yes. *You* can.

Pieter Yes.

Tom Then why are you still on your own?

Pieter Because I can see them all right, but they don't see me.

Tom That's tragic.

Pieter Well, Tom . . . like I always say: one jerk a day . . .

Tom And . . . what about going for it?

Pieter Beyond a certain age 'going for it' becomes a little distasteful.

Tom Oh, really?

Jan I've never had any complaints.

Tom So . . . if a man of forty-five sees another nice man of forty-five, he can't approach him because that would be distasteful?

Pieter I never see any nice men of forty-five.

Tom So beauty is youth?

Pieter I like young men, yes.

Tom How young?

Pieter Between eighteen and twenty-five.

Tom Oh.

Pieter It's not primarily physical.

Tom Oh.

Jan Oh, no?

Pieter No.

Jan I can't even exchange three sentences with a woman under thirty.

Pieter You can with one over thirty?

Tom Not primarily physical. What then?

Pieter They are still so beautifully what they are. Ambitious . . . egocentric . . . vain . . . self-centred, with such an absolute faith that everything will turn out well. That everything will work out for the best.

Jan Were we like that?

Tom Yes.

Pieter Yes.

Jan Tomorrow we'll know.

Tom What?

Jan If it's all turned out well. If everything's worked out for the best.

Pieter Are you going to talk to Conny?

Jan Not to Conny, to the whip. You are looking at a minister lying here.

Tom Would you finish an interview with Cloaca for us on camera just once? Just once? No, you can't. Of course you can't. Sorry.

Jan It's only a sort of sound? Something like 'Aloha,' but for us?

Tom A sort of sound?

Tom looks at Pieter: 'He doesn't know what it means.'

Jan It's just a made-up code word, isn't it? Isn't it? What is it, then? Does it mean something? It must be really filthy. Me, a cabinet minister. What a load of bull.

Tom That's good.

Jan My whole life I've been called 'promising'. It's probably right, but now I wonder, promising to whom?

Pieter I've never met anyone as ambitious as you. You've always been like that.

Jan So that's what you find so beautiful? Under thirty?

Pieter Not in your case. With you, ambition always had a very merciless edge to it.

Jan Come on . . . not now, surely. Now all I think is, in twenty years I'll be done with it. A farm in France, a boat on the Vecht, an apartment by a canal . . . and, God willing, not one more day of being 'promising'. In the morning, wander off down to the corner to buy a bit of cheese. Or bugger about a bit with the grapes . . . read a good book . . . maybe listen to a spot of Mahler . . . and then afterwards a liqueur.

Pieter A liqueur?

Jan Yes, crazy, eh?

Tom And are you planning to do all this all on your own or with us?

Jan That's funny. Conny said something like that too. Only with her it wasn't a question, it was an accusation: 'I don't fit into your future anywhere.' People seem to find it difficult to imagine that they might be important to me.

Pieter You've kept that well hidden.

Jan Have I become a complete shit?

Pieter Yes.

Tom Yes.

Jan Really? But . . . Maarten is surely a much bigger arsehole than I am?

Tom Yes.

Pieter Yes.

Jan lifts himself up with some difficulty. Tidies his hair a bit.

Jan You two have always been the softer of us. But . . . is that so much better? You went nuts because of it, and you're still alone. (*He walks through the room and sees his two friends sitting on the couch.*) Did I say that? Did I say that? . . . Oh! What a complete shit I am.

Pieter Is it going to work out with my Van Goppels, Tom?

Tom 'A day-dream of luxurious fun fur in elegant Arctic fox-style.'

Pieter Stop that nonsense, give me a straight answer for once.

Tom 'An elegant profile with a generous lapel and full cuffs. Slit pockets, and high, concealed vents.'

Pieter You'll have to pack in that job of yours. It's really not good for you.

Tom No. But what is good for me? What is?

Jan That Vermeulen . . . your boss . . . he's a rat. He gets a hundred thousand a year, he's incompetent and on the booze, favours his friends, so there's a pretty good chance that we'll get something on him that we'll be able to use. I've had all this checked out for you. So maybe I'm not such a terrible person after all.

Tom If Vermeulen confirms that the council gave those Van Goppels to you there's a great, or greater, chance that you can keep them.

Pieter But Vermeulen will never concede that.

Jan I've already got the thumbscrews for Vermeulen in my drawer, Piet. You should keep up. Before I go abroad I'll nail him for you.

Tom It would help if your colleagues confirm the gifts, in writing. So I've prepared a statement. (*For a moment he isn't able to find it in his pockets or in the plastic bag by the couch.*)

Pieter I don't have to take that round the office tomorrow, do I?

Tom I thought you might have a problem with that, so you give me their addresses, and I'll post them out the statement.

Jan Will we get to see these Van Goppels at some stage?

Pieter Some of them were hanging on the wall in my last house and the rest were stood on the floor.

Jan I never really looked at them.

Pieter You never really look at anything . . . they're all in a safe now.

Jan All eight?

Pieter All four.

Tom It was eight, wasn't it?

Pieter Yes, eight.

Jan But you said four.

Pieter Originally, there were eight.

Jan Originally?

Pieter I've had to sell four in the meantime.

Jan Are you taking the piss?

Pieter You surely don't think that I can afford to live here on my local-government salary? I had to move to a bigger house because I couldn't cram all my Van Goppels into that tiny broom-closet of mine. When they suddenly became worth so much I couldn't leave them plonked on the floor. That's really bad for paintings. So they all needed to be hung. And therefore, a bigger apartment . . . it just had to be. But, of course, I couldn't buy a bigger apartment without selling a couple of them. I came across a collector, an Australian private collector, and so . . . sold two . . . but then I ended up in a vicious circle. I had the space to hang the paintings, but I only had six of the Van Goppels left, and they kept rising in value, you have no idea what that sort of insurance costs and what they demand in terms of security measures! So, unfortunately, I had to sell another two. With pain in my heart. Pain in my heart.

Tom is still sitting with his arm around Pieter, but it appears as if he has heard none of this. Jan paces through the room.

Jan Bloody hell, Piet.

Pieter I had no choice. The paintings suddenly became worth so much. I hadn't expected that.

Tom Oh no? Hadn't you?

Pieter No! I'm not a dealer!

Tom It'll be a job and a half trying to explain that.

Maarten enters with a bag full of beer from the night shop.

Jan So the remaining four, they're in a safe?

Maarten Just now in the lift . . . on the street . . . in the night shop . . . on the street . . . in the lift . . . I thought: 'It's been too long. Between us. Things aren't as simple as they were.' I thought: 'Isn't it time I told them?'

Jan Maarten . . .

Maarten I have a problem.

Tom Yeh.

Maarten In the trouser department.

Jan Trouser department?

Maarten Maybe you have too, occasionally . . . for a day or two . . . but I've had it for a year already. And . . . with that whore . . . for a moment . . . I felt the sort of . . . stirrings . . . of a state of . . . being! Because . . . because . . . it's so much easier with that sort of woman. She wants money, she gets money, and then you get it. You just do it! It's so simple and uncomplicated!

Pieter Are you going to get sentimental about your limp dick? We can do without that.

Jan Where's this safe?

Pieter Now? We can't go there now.

Jan Suppose . . . things don't go well . . . and you have to give back all eight, what then?

Pieter A swift about-turn followed by my life in free fall. Sell the apartment . . . buy back the four Van Goppels I sold, with a loan. Because I couldn't cover the increase in value.

Maarten Impotent.

Pieter Yes, Maarten, we get it.

Darkness.

We hear strange music, for example 'Mockingbird' by Yo Yo Ma with Bobby McFerrin. An infectious sort of skipping music with an artistic tint on account of the cello. In terms of rhythm, it refers distantly to ska. Pieter enters the space doing skipping steps, in boxer shorts or a kimono, with a glass in his hand. He is deliriously happy and pretty drunk. With the remote control for the sound system in his other hand he keeps re-starting the song after a couple of beats. Moving through the space, he creates a cosy atmosphere with soft lighting. He is clearly relieved. Suddenly Maarten is standing in the doorway, asking all sorts of things, which cannot be heard. Initially, Pieter doesn't let his happiness be disturbed by Maarten's presence. Out of sheer necessity Maarten skips along for a couple of steps, but is clearly not in the mood for it.

Pieter You had the opening, didn't you? How did it go? I thought I'd give it a miss for a change. God, I've done well! How did it go? I couldn't come. I had some business to take care of. Pieter had to take care of business. I was really good, Maarten! Good! It's actually quite easy to get something done, quite easy. You have to . . . . do what Jan does . . . insinuate . . . I don't know . . . captivate . . . use a little blackmail. I didn't use that word, but it was there in the back of my mind. I managed to communicate it without saying the word.

Maarten What word, Pieter?

Pieter Suicide. Jesus, I was good! I went to work this morning with that letter of Tom's, which my colleagues had to sign. Stating that I was really given those eight Van Goppels. I was nervous and sick and trembling all day. I made some copies . . . waited for the break . . . I thought, I'll put one in everybody's pigeonhole. But I couldn't manage it. Four o'clock, everyone clearing up, five o'clock, everyone off home . . . I was disgusted with myself. Really. Cowardice has been hovering over me all my life. I go to a bar. Large brandy. Then on the bike. I think: I'll stick one through everybody's letter box and tomorrow I'll take the day off sick. And then on the way I almost threw up with misery, so I had another large brandy. I came to the first address, I wanted to stick the letter through the letter box, but they'd seen me. They opened the door. So . . . what could I say? I said: 'I've come to drop off something that needs a bit of clarification.' I go in. Children at the table with snakes and ladders. Can you believe it? In this day and age. Anyway, the kids are sat there playing snakes and ladders and I'm on the couch . . . explaining it all. Everything. Everyone's known about it for a while, of course: that I might have to give them all back, but I thought: think feelings. I began with a summary of the facts, then gradually I turned on the emotional thumbscrews, and started trembling and crying. Sobbing. The kids were completely stunned. A man sobbing next to your dad on the couch: it's a little different from sliding down a snake. And I pulled it off really well, Maarten! And slowly that word began to form in my mind, a sort of jumping-off point: suicide. Well . . . wonderful. Won-der-ful. He signed. That wanker from greater metropolitan policy, Theo Uilenburg . . . signed! Delirious! Back on my bike I was delirious. I couldn't pedal any longer. I actually had to stop. Well . . . I went round all twelve, all those other fools were home too, all sitting round their pans of spaghetti, and I got seven signatures! Seven out of twelve! So . . . everything's going to be fine. The paintings are mine. Jan's going to deal with Vermeulen . . . so . . . what can go wrong? I'd never have believed it. They're really mine now. I really had to wind myself up though, Maarten. I should never have sold them. I'm sorry that I did. Truly sorry. I could never buy them back. Impossible. If this hadn't worked out . . . I wouldn't have been able to go on. How could I have gone on? With Tom in that little room of his, with a conviction and debt repayments? How did it go, by the way? What are you doing here?

Maarten's answer is lost because Pieter has put 'Mockingbird' on again and cheerfully skips through the room. When he sees Maarten sitting there in despair with his head in his hands he turns the music off.

Pieter Didn't it go well?

Maarten Oh . . . yes.

Pieter Didn't you get a standing ovation?

Maarten Oh . . . yes.

Pieter So aren't you happy?

Maarten Well, to be honest, I thought, what's this actually about? I've never had any problem with that before. I've been infected with your judgements. Your middle-class, worn-out way of seeing.

Pieter But the performance – you're happy?

Maarten Well, I couldn't make any sense of it because the whole evening I was sat there looking through Jan's blinkered eyes. And yes, of course it's all a contrivance if your cultural touchstone is watching *The Bold and the Beautiful* every day. Then Laura. Boy . . . I . . . was twisting in my seat.

Pieter Was she extremely naked?

Maarten It's all about losing your virginity. That's what the scene's about. The words don't matter, they're deliberately meant not to be understood, what is important is that the girl loses her physical and spiritual virginity to the man. She becomes an adult and a woman.

Pieter Oh, dear.

Maarten And the thing was . . . I wasn't able to come up with anything . . . Laura thought the image up herself . . . as a metaphor for the loss of virginity. Very, very beautiful. She is really very good.

Pieter It didn't involve litres of blood and that sort of thing?

Maarten That's the first thing you'd think of . . . that she'd stand up and walk across the stage leaving a trail of blood behind her, and we did try that, but it didn't work very well.

Pieter Oh, dear.

Maarten If you'd have seen it, then you would have thought it was beautiful.

Pieter I think I'm going to sit down.

Maarten She . . . Laura is completely smeared with make-up, brown make-up, and is therefore a metaphor for the oppression of woman.

Pieter Oh . . . right, the oppression of woman. Does that bother you, then?

Maarten So . . . she's naked, but she's covered in brown make-up from head to toe. And then she encounters the man . . . and while he verbally takes her virginity, surprises, or rapes her, say, he picks up a garden hose . . .

Pieter Is that a metaphor too, the garden hose?

Maarten A hose, and he squirts her totally naked. Beautiful. Her white skin exposed and quivering. People were moved.

Pieter Jan too.

Maarten Conny was really moved.

Pieter And Jan?

Maarten No idea. Afterwards we couldn't find him. We were waiting for him backstage with champagne . . . but no Jan. Laura was in tears . . . he is her father, after all. We wait . . . it really brought the mood down. Conny was proud . . . but there was no Jan, no Daddy. Then Conny said that he might have already left.

Pieter Yes . . . well . . . he certainly isn't here.

Maarten I have to speak to him.

Pieter Yes . . . but he isn't here.

Maarten The trouble is . . . Laura. Laura wouldn't accept it. She's just like Jan. She exploded when she heard that he'd already left. She's okay now though, Laura.

Pieter Well . . . that's between father and daughter, Maarten. I . . . will you just leave? I was in a good mood a moment ago.

Maarten Laura is very loyal to me. She won't take this from her father. So . . . I have to speak to Jan before Laura does. To . . . explain a few things.

It takes some time for the penny to drop with Pieter.

Pieter But . . . you're impotent, aren't you?

Maarten Yes. I, er . . . what I said yesterday. I can't do it any more. The act itself is still a turn-on, but all the crap afterwards, Pieter. It drives me crazy. There is always . . . it doesn't matter who you're with . . . there is always a price to pay. The thought of it just makes me limp. All that interminable crap. Love for ever, friends for ever, some kind of artistic emotional union for ever . . . all because you happen to have screwed someone. Naturally you have to take them to Mexico for six weeks because 'It'll be cool'. Awful things. They do really awful things. One of them tells me I'm not allowed to talk to the other, another that I'm not allowed to rehearse with the previous one. And yet another tells me I have to drop by every Friday because it was good a couple of times on a Friday. Come on! Let things be what they are! Why can't these women let things be if there's nothing wrong! Why does it always have to be more and more, when more and more is by definition less! Why is that! Now they're all getting broody too. Nature calls! The biological clock is ticking! My arse, Pieter, my arse. Biological clock? Bullshit. All those women just want children to disguise the total social failures that they have turned into. Do I have to be punished for that? And so when there is some whore wandering about here, who is already paid for, a simple, clear, arrangement with no ifs and buts . . . then yes . . . then . . . yes . . . I get excited. To me it's wonderfully straightforward.

Pieter Did you really do it with Laura?

Maarten Laura is another story. Laura is the first, maybe the only one, who could do that. She has something . . . Jan-ish . . . good sex, and that's it. Never wants to sleep over. Laura is really okay. But now she's getting emotional, yes. She thinks Jan's insulted me. Not her. But me. That may be true, but I really don't want her to go apeshit with him. If she gets stuck into her father . . . and she can . . . then . . . you know . . . Jan'll get to hear things, and it would be best if I were to prepare the ground beforehand.

Pieter Maarten . . . Laura is the child of your friend.

Maarten I wouldn't say child.

Pieter Laura is eighteen.

Maarten Come on, Pieter, age doesn't mean anything these days.

Pieter You shouldn't have done it.

Maarten And what about Jan? A letter box isn't safe with him about. You should talk to Conny sometime. I didn't want to do it, I told you, didn't I? I can't do it any more. Only with Laura, it's . . . different. To her sex is something so straightforward. She just jumped me. No chat beforehand, no drink. It doesn't interest her. And yes . . . it was an eye-opener to me. Let's just say it worked.

Pieter I've never shown a friend the door, but I'm going to right now. You need to go. I don't want to be here when Jan sees you. Go, Maarten.

Maarten Yes. Okay, then.

Suddenly Jan is standing in the doorway.

Jan Don't go.

Maarten Jan . . .

Jan Maarten.

Pieter Where's Tom?

Jan I lost him. Lost him somewhere in the centre of town. Maybe he couldn't stand it any longer, I wouldn't be surprised. God . . . I was in a state.

Maarten Jan.

Jan And I still am. Still am. We walked, Tom and I . . . walked and walked, and suddenly he was gone. Poor Tom . . . God . . . you did warn me, Maarten.

Maarten Oh?

Jan I was taken totally unawares. And then I saw her and suddenly I knew how things were.

Pieter Where's Tom? Tom still isn't totally right. Where is he?

Jan I don't know. I really don't know. I was walking around like a fool, snivelling and carrying on . . . and suddenly he was gone . . . the way she was just sitting there.

Pieter You've got to look for him. Dickhead! He isn't allowed to go into town on his own.

Jan Tom is forty-two.

Pieter And confused!

Jan Me too! Me too, Piet. I looked; you said, 'She'll be sitting in row one,' but she wasn't there. She was in the side balcony. Godalmightyjesus . . . that beautiful suit she had on. Is it new?

Maarten Eh . . .

Jan Beautiful! And she looked as if she'd lost ten kilos. And that hair. Has she . . . been to the hairdresser or something?

Maarten Conny.

Jan Yes, Conny. Conny. In that suit, so proud and confident with Teddy, Bram and Micha beside her. And seeing those lovely children. It was because I didn't know it was her, it was a bit dark and I didn't have my glasses on, and because I thought I was looking at a woman that I didn't know, I suddenly saw it. Jackie Onassis. I had a photo of her in my room as a boy, the one with Jackie and the children standing at Kennedy's grave . . . I was in love with Jackie . . . and only at that moment did I see that it was Conny. Conny is my first love! Conny is Jackie.

Pieter And you are Jan F. Kennedy.

Jan I thought: there's my wife, there's the mother of my children, there's my family, tomorrow I'll be a minister and that minister belongs with that family. What in God's name am I doing? Then the play was about to start. I was completely . . . you know . . . I . . . as if I were seeing her for the first time. What a wonderful woman. Exactly the sort of woman for me. And then Laura . . .

Maarten Yes . . .

Jan I went to pieces, almost died. Naturally, I couldn't sit there in tears, so I held it in, but Tom who was sitting next to me said: 'Jan, these chairs are all bolted together, the whole row is shaking because of you. So just go ahead and cry.' I'm sorry, Maarten . . . I should have trusted you. Oh God . . . the vision . . . of that beautiful young woman's body, stripped naked by that water. I . . . well . . . it was beautiful . . . and that water all around her. Pieter . . . you should have seen it . . . first she was covered with brown make-up, then that was hosed away so that she was surrounded by a pool of reddish-brown . . . well . . . blood, let's say. Very beautiful, very, very beautiful, Maarten.

Maarten Thank you, Jan.

Jan I should have trusted you, of course. Sorry.

Maarten Well . . . fathers . . .

Jan After the applause I went up to Conny in the foyer, I wanted to give her a kiss, lift her up, take her in my arms . . . my wife, my girl . . . but . . . she was standing there so upright, with a child in each hand. So I didn't dare to. Honestly. She said: 'Sweetheart, are you okay?' I said: 'I didn't recognise you for a moment.' She said: 'I could see that from the way you were looking at me.' And she laid her hand on my arm and said very softly: 'The way that you came into my life twenty-five years ago is the best thing that ever happened to me, and the best present you have given me since is to leave again. It is so wonderful that you had the courage. You were right. It was finished. It was really finished.'

Maarten Oh.

Pieter Oh?

Jan She walked away, with the children, they waved back, happily. ''Bye, Daddy' And then . . . it was as though an invisible hand went 'snip'. With huge sharp scissors. I heard the sound. 'Snip' echoing in my head. Then everything went black for a second, and then in large bright letters I saw: 'Jan Korenman, Secretary of State for Foreign Affairs, four children, divorced.'

Pieter And Tom was standing next to you the whole time.

Jan Tom took me outside. At home I had asked for a little breathing space . . . and now she says she doesn't expect to see me back.

Pieter You didn't ask for a little breathing space, you stuck a meat fork in her face.

Jan Sorry. Sorry.

Pieter So . . . you'll have to call an estate agent.

Jan Yes. Sorry.

Maarten Jan.

Jan Maarten.

Pieter Tom.

Tom is standing in the doorway. With a can of Coke and two children's straws.

Tom Cloaca! Coke anyone? (*He throws the can to the lads and walks towards the toilet with the straws.*)

Pieter Not in my toilet! Tom! Not in my toilet!

Jan What.

Pieter I don't want it. You can't handle it. Do you want to go crazy again? Do you want to end up back on that roof in a Batman cape?

Tom returns. But he has snorted something quickly.

Pieter Where were you? What are you doing? What do you want?

Tom I've had a think about it. And I've worked it out.

Pieter Have you been using? Let me see your nose.

Tom Yes, of course I've been using. I want to get back to being myself, okay? A little peace of mind. You are all so in the present. You, with you . . . it's understandable, Piet . . . I'm helping . . . with your problem. As you asked me to. Okay.

Pieter Seven signatures, Tom.

Tom Okay. Okay. (*He hugs Pieter as a sort of sacred gesture.*) Good. That's good. And now . . . everyone go home. Not you, Piet, because you live here, but Maarten and Jan . . . you have to go. I've just got out of the nut-house . . . which seems to have slipped your minds, and nobody seems sorry about it, nobody seems to realise how intensely alone you are when you're imprisoned inside your own fear . . . that's what I've had to deal with . . . I don't want to be resentful . . . I probably did it all to myself . . . destroyed my own mind . . . but now I'm well again and I want to stay that way. And if the four of us stay together like this, then it's all going to go wrong again. We are in . . . we . . . are in a sort of vicious circle of negativity. And that's not the same as bad luck. Bad luck's okay and that's why Pieter's problem is for real and almost resolved . . . but, Jan, your situation makes me nervous. So now I've decided: I don't need to see it, I don't have to become involved in it and I certainly don't want to help to solve it. Do you know what I think? It's terrible. It's fucking terrible.

Jan Tom . . . it's all right. Calm down. It's all been sorted out.

Tom We . . . Piet and I . . . we're okay. We're going to be all right. But you, Jan . . . and you, Maarten – let me put it this way: I can't be here for you any more. Sorry.

Maarten What did you think of the play? Or was it just shite again?

Tom No.

Maarten Did it move you?

Tom With Jan sat next to me feeling for the whole row, I wasn't really able to concentrate, but it did occur to me: Maarten isn't happy.

Maarten nods and walks across the room to make a call on his mobile.

Jan Tomorrow I'm going to buy an apartment, whatever's on offer, I'll hardly be there anyway. Tomorrow I'll be gone.

Tom I was there when you let Conny go . . . don't forget that. It makes no difference to me. You can do whatever you like. Do what the hell you like.

Jan Let Conny go? You heard what she said? She doesn't expect to see me at home any more. Everyone's doing so much better now that I've gone.

Tom Dickhead.

Jan What?

Tom Dickhead! If you'd gone down on your knees. Offered her roses . . . apologised . . . kidnapped her even. Dragged her out of the theatre. Grabbed her, danced with her. Taken her out to dinner. Driven her to the coast. Carried her in your arms. If you'd said, 'How beautiful you look,' if you'd kissed your children. Or said, 'I'll die without you, I want to come home.' But you just stood there looking at your own family like a woman watching a football game. If you'd said something! Done something!

Jan It didn't occur to me. But I can still talk to her?

Tom Dickhead.

Jan She said: 'It's a good thing you buggered off, because it was finished between us.'

Tom 'Still talk to her?' It's too late for that.

Jan So?

Tom Do I have to explain *everything*? She kept on standing there! So . . . you still had a chance. She was waiting for something. From you. Dickhead. She stood looking at you for a full minute. And you said nothing. Only at that point, at that very moment, did she decide that it was good that you'd buggered off.

Jan Should I have said: 'Conny, can I come back to my own house?'

Tom To you and the children.

Jan To you and the children?

Tom Can I come back to you and the children? Yes.

Jan Oh. So that was what I should have said.

Tom Yes . . . and then she could have set out her conditions. 'You have to spend more time at home, and not have any more affairs . . .'

Jan Okay, okay, okay, okay! I didn't say anything! I didn't say anything!

Tom No, you didn't. And I don't want to walk around this city with you any more, listening to that snivelling. I don't want it. We have to go forwards, Piet and I. You two are just dragging us back.

Maarten I'm heading off. My people are waiting for me. It's my party.

Pieter Good.

Maarten Tom . . . sorry . . . that I wasn't there. Then.

Tom And you'll never get the chance again.

Pieter Oh no? If you're going to be back to sticking something up your nose every day, then he'll get that chance quicker than you think. Jan is buying an apartment tomorrow and for the time being you are staying in the guest room.

Tom Good. Good. And now the case. Our case. Our case is still not completely settled. Jan? You still have to deal with Vermeulen.

Jan Yes.

Tom Is there any movement there?

Jan Yes.

Maarten I'm er . . . going. Bit stupid not being at your own first-night party.

Pieter Yes. Enjoy your party. Say hello to Laura.

Jan Laura. Can you explain it to her, Maarten?

Maarten Yes.

Pieter Just go. Go and explain it.

Jan I can stay here tonight, can't I? I've got that appointment with the whip tomorrow.

Maarten Well . . . 'bye. Shall we . . . kick a ball around sometime, lads? Soon? I've got some free time now. Tomorrow? The park?

Pieter Yes, okay, Maarten. The park tomorrow.

Maarten leaves forlornly.

Tom Do you know which case I'd like to take on? The greatest complaint ever . . . against the United States of America and Russia. The biggest fraud of all times . . . wonderful. And what is this case? The moon landings . . . total nonsense. It's impossible. It's simply impossible. Bear with me for a moment . . . What proof do we actually have that they really took place? Some vague pictures of a couple of men floating around in thick suits who can't be identified, and a couple of foggy pictures of a rocket that could just as well have been made of papier mâché, which they burned up one kilometre above the earth. All fake. Billions and billions have ended up in the pockets of the world mafia because of this, and do you know what's happened to that money?

Pieter No, and we don't want to know. You're starting to crack up. (*He points at his head.*) Go to sleep, Tom. Jan, off the couch.

Tom Sleep? Sleep? I'll just take a little stroll, I think.

Pieter Wanker. You cowardly wanker. Why can't you just say no for once?

Tom Tomorrow.

Tom leaves. Pieter and Jan remain still for some time.

Jan Tomorrow.

Pieter Tomorrow.

A long period of darkness

For the first time a scene takes place during the day. Perhaps, if it is possible, there should be light coming in from outside. In any case, the scene on the stage is somewhat 'colder' than it was previously. Tom is sleeping on the couch, beneath a thin blanket. Jan has just come in. He gathers some of his things together. Or, alternatively, he comes out of the bathroom and stuffs them into the bag and the suitcase that he arrived with. He goes over and sits next to Tom and looks at him for quite a while. Maybe smokes a cigarette. With his jacket on, bag and case ready for departure. Jan starts speaking to Tom, although he has not visibly woken up.

Jan Things have turned out differently than I'd expected. And they keep turning out differently. But this won't only have consequences for me. We'll have to scrub the whole thing, Tom. Scrub the whole thing.

Tom wakes up.

I can't allow my term of office to start like this.

Tom Jan.

Jan Tom.

Tom And?

Jan It's going to be very difficult. And you'll have to help me.

Tom The FO?

Jan No Tom, not the FO, nor the Treasury.

Tom Employment then?

Jan I set someone on that prick Vermeulen.

Tom And?

Jan He broke like a flower in the morning dew. He'd conceded that the whole lot was a gift within a quarter of an hour. He'll get his handshake pay-off and end up somewhere checking the duty on gin, for all I know. Anyway, he's gone.

Tom He's been dealt with. Good.

Jan But I'm not going to do anything with the information. And you're going to tell Pieter.

Tom And . . . what has brought this change of heart, Minister?

Jan I've been appointed . . . to a post . . . where, let's just say, I am withdrawing from the whole damned affair.

Tom The case is settled. What do you mean, you're withdrawing? That's impossible.

Jan A lot more things happen, which shouldn't, than you might imagine.

Tom You're in this. You agreed. You've helped.

Jan Oh no.

Tom Oh yes. It's almost settled now. You know what those paintings mean to him, don't you?

Jan No. I don't know anything at all about any Van Goppels.

Tom Oh yes, you do know.

Jan Those fucking things are going back to the council.

Tom Have you been put under pressure?

Jan Oh, no.

Tom What difference does it make, then? From now on you'll be a long way away most of the time.

Jan No. I won't.

Tom And he can't give them back, he's sold four of them already.

Jan That's unfortunate. But it's not my problem.

Tom And that's what you're going to tell Pieter? You've got the nerve to say that to him?

Jan No. You are going to say it.

Tom I'll send him to you.

Jan I've rented an apartment, on the other side of town. I never stayed here. I've never even been here.

Tom Listen a minute, Jan: we're arseholes, but we did say that we'd work this out for him. We promised. That means something. And we're sticking to it.

Jan Game over.

Tom What went on at the whip's?

Jan How should I know? Somebody with more air miles ended up at the FO.

Tom Have you been passed over?

Jan No. Deposited. Dumped.

Tom Not foreign affairs.

Jan Culture.

Tom Culture? You? Secretary of State?

Jan Well, minister. A done deal.

Tom You?

Jan Culture, God. What a let-down. I will have lots of free time now, though. So maybe now Conny would reconsider.

Tom That's why you're dropping Pieter?

Jan Yes. Of course. It might be a joke of a job, but I can't start it with my head in a noose. 'Brand new minister defends homosexual college friend who misappropriated eight works of art from the council.'

Tom Misappropriated? What crap are you spouting now?

Jan Goodbye, Tom. This is it. Goodbye, Tom. (*He picks up his things and walks to the door.*) Cloaca . . . does it actually really mean anything?

Tom No.

A long period of darkness.

Tom and Maarten are together in the apartment. A sense of anticipation.

Maarten So my mate Jan has the power to decide whether or not I'm allowed to make theatre the way I want to.

Tom Yes.

Maarten Maybe I'll have to put a bit of distance between myself and Laura, then.

Tom Pieter's going to be home any moment.

Maarten Cowardly wanker, Jan.

Tom How um . . . are we going to tell him this?

Maarten Do we *have* to?

Tom Yes.

Maarten He does have all those signatures, after all?

Tom It's not enough. We needed an acknowledgement from Vermeulen. That was in Jan's hands. And it was going well, too.

Maarten Will . . . Pieter have to sell this place?

Tom He'll have to live in a rented room for the rest of his life, and repay his debt until he dies. He has to buy back four paintings. The owner can ask what he wants for them.

Maarten Pieter's caught between a rock and a hard place. And what a hard place it is.

Tom I'll never drop him.

Maarten What are you going to tell him?

Tom That I'll always keep in touch with him.

Maarten You'd really like me to stay, wouldn't you?

Tom Jan has put a knife in my hand.

Maarten How . . . maybe it'd be best . . . just to tell him straight how things are.

Tom Yes.

Maarten Tom?

Tom Yes?

Maarten Is there no other way?

Tom Litigate. Hope for a settlement.

Maarten You have to be the type for that. Would Pieter be able to cope?

Tom thinks 'No.'

Tom Can I just . . . (*He stands up.*)

Maarten Don't go now! Don't leave!

Tom Twenty minutes.

Maarten No! Tom!

Tom I'm going to tell him. I am. I just have to go out for a while first. I'll be right back.

Maarten remains alone.

A long period of darkness.

Maarten Pieter.

Pieter Maarten. Isn't Tom home? I mean here?

Maarten He's just popped out.

Pieter So . . . why are you here, then? Something's different. Jan's gone.

Maarten Yes. Jan's gone.

Pieter Gone for good? His things too?

Maarten Yes.

Pieter Bizarre . . . oh . . . oh . . . wait a second. I heard he got Culture. Jan got Culture.

Maarten Yes. I think because he actually went to the theatre three times in one year.

Pieter It's like I'm visiting you.

Maarten Yes.

Pieter And you weren't expecting me.

Maarten Yes.

Pieter Well, come on, Maarten . . . out with it.

Maarten Yes . . . you think I'm a dickhead. It's true.

Pieter Did he just leave? Or will he be back soon? To explain?

Maarten I'm not a coward. I'm still here.

Pieter No, that's me. I'm the coward. Always have been.

Maarten No, not you. Jan.

Pieter Oh. Then he isn't coming back. He isn't just moving his things and then coming back to go out to dinner with us. No.

Maarten I'm your friend. I have to tell you this. That's what friends do.

Pieter Jan has really gone, then. No message?

Maarten Jan has gone. He was never here.

Pieter Ah ha. Was never here. I think this is all leading up to something, Maarten. I'm beginning to fear the worst.

Maarten Look . . .

Pieter I don't think I want to hear this.

Maarten I have to tell you. I'm your friend.

Pieter You're going to tell me he's dropping me. That's what I'm thinking, but I hope I'm mistaken.

Maarten doesn't respond.

Because . . . Culture . . . all his things gone . . . and the fact that you are sitting here. There is something you have to tell me.

Maarten Yes.

Pieter I don't want to hear this. And it can't be true, because you aren't the one who'd tell me. Tom would never agree.

Maarten I. I'm telling you. Because I can tell you.

Pieter Well . . . I really don't think that Tom . . . that Tom would agree to this.

Maarten Tom doesn't have to agree to anything. Tom has gone. Had to. Suddenly.

Pieter begins to understand the way things are.

Pieter Go on then, Maarten. Tell me.

Maarten Jan thinks . . . Jan . . . Look, Jan is first and foremost an opportunist and he is also immensely ambitious.

Pieter Nothing new there.

Maarten Jan is not proceeding with Vermeulen.

Pieter Not proceeding?

Maarten Jan's dropping you.

Pieter Yes.

Maarten Did you know?

Pieter No. Oh, no. Not until this moment. Now that you've told me. Anything else?

Maarten That I'm not going to drop you.

Pieter Only I've already been dropped.

Maarten That I'll be here for you, I mean.

Pieter That's good of you.

Maarten understands that his 'heroic deed' has not been appreciated.

Maarten Tom'll be back soon. Tom'll be here soon.

Pieter So that's how it goes. That's how it goes.

A long silence.

The most wonderful thing about Van Goppel is that he was always in an extreme emotional state before starting to paint. It was essential. I didn't know that at first, even though I'd already seen it in his work. That heightened sensitivity . . . I've never experienced anything like it, though I have some sense of how it might feel.

Maarten Yes.

Pieter And it was essential for him to reach that state of extremity.

Maarten Yes. Yes. Yes.

Pieter How does one do that? How does one free oneself so much without disappearing into chaos? How does one do that? And why have I never been able to?

Maarten I think this is going to have quite serious financial consequences for you. I can lend you some money. A long-term, interest-free loan. A hundred thousand or so. Think about it.

Pieter Because he painted and painted, layer upon layer, and never knew when it was finished. And he was often depressed.

Maarten I wouldn't start by giving everything back immediately.

Pieter No. Oh, no. That's impossible.

Maarten Litigation is also an option.

Pieter Give everything back?

Maarten Tom said something like that, yes.

Pieter It isn't about those daubs of paint. It's about what they make you feel. That's what I loved about them. The emotion that the paintings stirred in me. An intuition of . . .

He walks into the bathroom.

At last, Maarten. At last I get to express an emotion. Make an emotion tangible. Van Goppel didn't know when something was finished. I do.

Darkness.

Maarten is sitting on the couch. Tom comes in. He's been snorting.

Tom Done already? And?

Maarten looks at Tom for a long time.

Maarten So beautifully put.

Tom What?

Maarten About . . . I can't remember what it was about now. But so beautifully put.

Tom Have you told him yet?

Maarten Yes.

Tom And then?

Maarten Nothing.

Tom What do you mean?

Maarten Nothing.

Tom What do you mean?

Maarten You weren't there.

Tom No.

Maarten Nor was Jan. Something had to be said. So I said it.

Tom I told you: 'I'll be right back.' Did you tell him that? You told him.

Maarten And then he quietly went to the bathroom, very quietly. I thought: 'Naturally, he's confused. He needs to be alone for a while. Let his feelings out. Cry, maybe.' I heard the tap. The bath. Him getting into the bath. I was waiting out here for you.

Tom Oh, no.

Maarten And then I thought: 'This is taking an awful long time. He's going to do something to himself.' I thought: 'I've got to try to do something.' I thought: 'He's already done it.' That's how it was. Something like that. And then I found him.

Silence. Tom walks over to the bathroom. Remains standing in the doorway.

Maarten Tom?

Tom Yes?

Maarten Strange, such clarity. While you are dying.

Tom Yes.

End.